饮水思源

ideogram

The Prosperous Peasant

Five Secrets of
Fortune & Fulfillment from the
Samurai's Temple School

Tim Clark & Mark Cunningham

The Prosperous Peasant
Tim Clark and Mark Cunningham

Copyright ©2007 by Tim Clark
Design: Keiko Onodera
Editing: James Reid Harrison

Published by Ideogram
4110 SE Hawthorne Blvd. No. 322
Portland, OR 97214-5246
503.238.2034 phone
503.238.2054 fax
www.ideogram.us

Books are available in customized editions and at quantity discounts for special events or for educational use. Please call or write the publisher for details.

Acknowledgements
Chapter 5 quotes several edited paragraphs of text from *The Life of Toyotomi Hideyoshi*, originally written in 1888 by Walter Dening. The final third of Chapter 5 is adapted from the short story *Honest Kyūsuke* by Miyamori Asataro. Chapter 8 is an edited version of the complete short story entitled *Ungo-Zenji*, also by Miyamori. Chapter 11 is an edited summary of the 1899 work entitled *Bushido* by Nitobe Inazo.

Notice of Rights
All rights reserved. No part of this book may be reproduced or transmitted in any form or by any means, electronic, mechanical, photocopying, recording, or otherwise, without the prior written permission of the publisher. For information on obtaining permission for reprints and excerpts, write to permissions@ideogram.us.

ISBN 978-0-9800026-0-7

Printed and bound in the United States of America

For Ray and Lina, with love and best wishes for your own fortune and fulfillment.

Contents

1 In Search of the Prosperous Peasant 1

2 The Road to Nagahama 13

3 The Samurai's Secrets 31

4 The Temple School 59

5 Gratitude Attracts Luck:
The Scroll of Fortune 83

6 Know Your Gift:
The Potter's Counsel 107

7 Conceivable Means Achievable:
Nobunaga the "Fool" 119

8 Effort Determines Results:
The Vengeful Priest 137

9 Collaboration Breeds Success:
The Guns of Tanegashima 153

10 Hideyoshi and the Age of
Warring Clans 175

11 Bushido 181

Afterword 207
About the authors 211

饮水思源

When you drink from a stream, remember the spring.
Chinese proverb

決意 1

In Search of the Prosperous Peasant

*J*iro, the eighteen-year-old pride of Miwa Village, was downhearted. With a heavy sigh, he hoisted yet another sheaf of rice seedlings to his broad shoulders and trotted toward the flooded paddies. The late-day sun beat down upon his sweat-soaked head.

Laboring villagers admired the handsome youth as he passed. Older men gazed enviously at his limber gait; young girls glimpsed the powerful tanned legs moving beneath his hemp robe and blushed; married women smiled knowingly at one another, and glanced at his intended among the maidens.

Jiro noticed none of this, for he was deep in thought. An image from his dream of the night before haunted him strangely—he'd beheld himself an old man with white hair and tired eyes. Why so troubled by a dream? he asked himself now. Finishing the May planting is a time for celebration.

Lost in his own thoughts, Jiro approached a line of stooped girls rhythmically pressing sprouted seedlings into the soft, wet mud. They sang a lilting worksong, which only underscored his melancholy mood:

> *Seedlings won't you ripen*
> *Quickly, seedlings, quickly*
> *Yes, soon ripen green*

Seventeen-year-old Shizue, the oldest and prettiest of the maidens, gave Jiro a shy smile as he tossed his sheaf to the mud a half-step behind her, so she could grab the next plant without breaking the pace of her work. He would have thrilled at their wordless connection, were his heart not aching with a longing for change—change he sensed must come this very day.

Jiro trotted back to the mud embankment, where he paused to gaze across the lush green terrain he'd known since his earliest youth. To the west Mount Yoro rose above the fertile country, its peak tinged golden by the falling sun.

My future looms before me as clearly as that mountain, thought Jiro, but so much less remarkable. I'll marry Shizue, who's beautiful indeed—but what will we make of our life? Together we'll build a wood-framed house with walls of plaster and straw. Its thatched roof will shed the summer rains and winter snows. From May through September, we'll continue the endless cycle of rice planting, tending, and harvest.

In the cooling months of late fall, Shizue will spin and weave, and I'll gather fuel for the approaching winter: wood from the hills nearby, leaves from the bamboo grove behind our home. The village will harvest millet, persimmons, and mushrooms, and I'll fish. Rice threshing will follow, then harvesting of potatoes, taro root, cabbage, and the white *daikon* radishes that grow to the size of a man's foot. In the winter months, I'll set to work repairing the farm tools recent harvests have blunted, and I'll carve building beams—and maybe brew a little *sake* if tax payments to the Oda clan leave enough extra rice.

Early spring will mean vegetable planting, fern shoot gathering, wheat field tending, and fertilizing the mulberry fields. Shizue will make hair oil. There will be children: a boy and a girl, I hope, for though Japan favors young men, I want to see Shizue's beauty and gentle temperament reflected in a daughter. Then, someday, my children will be grown, and I can …

I can what? Jiro asked himself. Do I have nothing to live for but tradition? Am I destined to spend my whole life in Miwa, never to see the world beyond, never to stray from the path laid forth for me by generations past?

Such thoughts seemed to cast a gloom across the colorful spring day.

The noise of galloping horses woke Jiro from his brooding. Three mounted samurai, resplendent in battle armor, had cantered up to a group of workers across the field.

Genzaemon, son of the village headman, bowed to the riders, all Oda vassals. Jiro was too far away to hear the words passing between them. Genzaemon signalled for the laborers to rest, and they straightened up, mopping their brows. Children brought them bamboo cups brimming with cool water.

The sound of footsteps reached Jiro's ears. He turned to see his best friend, Gonsuke, approaching, a smile on his broad face. As always, the small birthmark beneath Gonsuke's left eye seemed to enhance his smile, just as it accentuated his scowl in the darker moments Jiro had shared with him.

"Working hard?" Gonsuke asked with a laugh. He was recently married, with his first child on the way, and his disposition was even sunnier than usual. Like all peasants, he went by a single name.

Jiro greeted his old comrade with a slap on the back. "Plenty of work as always! But as always I'm going nowhere."

Gonsuke plunked himself down on the embankment. "Rest yourself!" he said, and tossed Jiro a *nigiri* rice ball.

Jiro sat. His teeth sank into the tart pickled plum at the center of the *nigiri*. He chewed, brooding. Gonsuke studied him intently.

"You're thoughtful today. What's the trouble? Distracted as always by Shizue's beauty, no doubt."

The younger man looked up, too somber to return his friend's smile. "Tell me, Gonsuke, what's the meaning of work whose only reward is more work?"

Gonsuke was silent.

"We labor hard," said Jiro, "but does it raise us above the lot of our fathers, and our fathers' fathers? We plow, sow, and tend the paddies, then harvest, heckle, and store the rice. Lord Nobunaga takes from one-fifth to one-half in taxes, depending on the richness of the harvest, then through the winter months we ready ourselves for another cycle of seasons, and more backbreaking labor."

"What're you saying, Jiro?"

"I had a dream last night, Gonsuke. I was old, very old, with long white eyebrows. Years of labor had bent my back, and my fingers were bony and gnarled. I was still a farmer, exactly as I am now."

Gonsuke frowned. "Those days are a long way off, Jiro. You're the pride of Miwa. All the youngsters look up to you."

Jiro shook his head. "Look at those samurai over there. They thunder about, free to travel anywhere and serve whomever they choose. They're not shackled to the land!" He rolled the plum pit around in his cheeks, sucking off the last shreds of tangy pulp, then spat the stone in an impressive arc. It fell to the ground with a soft *thup* fully twelve feet away.

"You envy the samurai?" Gonsuke's brow creased in a worried grimace. "Admiring them is one thing, but envy? Think about it, Jiro. Are they really free? Each one reports to Nobunaga, and each must lay down his life if commanded. Is that freedom?"

"I don't envy their willingness to die," sighed Jiro. "But if they distinguish themselves in battle, they're well rewarded. And they can choose whatever life they want. If one master displeases them, they can serve another. Or abandon the sword and become farmers, craftsmen, or merchants under their family names. That's the freedom I want, Gonsuke—the freedom to rise in the world based on my own abilities—nothing more, nothing less." Jiro's voice quavered with pent-up emotion.

"You've never talked like this before."

"I've never felt like this, Gonsuke. But that dream was a warning—that I'm standing on a cusp in life. One way leads down a safe but unadventurous path. Another could begin a thrilling journey."

Jiro grew quiet. Only now, as he gave them voice, had he fully formed his thoughts, and the force behind them caught him by surprise.

The friends sat wordlessly for several long moments, staring across the paddy. The declining sun was turning the watery fields to a sheet of bronze. Finally Gonsuke broke the silence.

"Were this a just world, Jiro, men like you and me could choose our destinies. You could live by your talents as a carpenter. I could be a merchant. But what's the point of thinking that way? Each of us is born into his lot. Samurai are born to samurai families. Sons of merchants become merchants. And sons of peasants, Jiro, become farmers like you and me. That's how it's always been."

"But must it remain that way?" cried Jiro. "Who knows what the future holds? Do you believe your destiny is written on a temple scroll? Are the samurai so different from you and me? What natural law decrees one man a noble and another a vassal? Birthright doesn't guarantee ability. Why, everyone knows the deposed *shogun's* as stupid as a goat!"

"Shh!" Gonsuke cautioned, for Jiro's rising voice had begun to turn the heads of a few villagers. "We'll both regret it if those sword-wielding brutes hear your insulting talk."

The two friends glanced at the trio of samurai, who had finished their dealings with Genzaemon and were readying their horses to depart.

Jiro drew closer to Gonsuke, and lowered his voice. "Don't you want to see the world beyond this village? Aren't you curious about the wonders lying across the shores of Lake Biwa? In Kyoto, Echizen, and Musashi? Once, when I was a boy, I ate a mandarin from Satsuma Province. I'll never forget how sweet it was—I thought my tongue would melt! I want to taste those sweet mandarins again, and be free to walk the beaches of Tanegashima, where the red-haired barbarians first set foot upon our islands. Instead I'm chained to a peasant's life!"

Gonsuke sat staring into the hardened mud. He spoke softly. "I've thought that way too, Jiro—more times than you know. But I've never told anyone. To be honest, it troubles me to hear you say these things."

"But why?" Jiro brightened at his friend's confession. "Why not admit your deep longing to become a merchant and act upon it? Why pretend we're content to slave in the fields? If we fail to grasp our purpose today, where will we be ten or twenty years from now?"

"True enough," Gonsuke agreed. "But remember, I'm older. Unlike you, the path I trod seems deeper carved every day. My wife's expecting, and I have to plan for a family, not just for two."

"All the more reason to act now!" cried Jiro, leaping to his feet and sweeping his arms toward the south, where Ise Bay embraced the green waters of the Pacific Ocean. "Even as we speak, this village is drawing me toward a fate I can't accept. When will we seize destiny, Gonsuke, if not today?"

"You sound like a poet, my friend." Gonsuke hammered a fist upon the ground. "But you're right. By the Buddha, this talk does me good!" For a moment he gazed pensively across the plains leading west toward Kyoto and Osaka. Then he looked up at Jiro with a smile. "Priests speak of two kinds of study: whereby one learns skills, and whereby one learns how to learn. We haven't learned how to seek our prosperity, our happiness, simply because we haven't studied the problem."

"Yes," agreed Jiro. "Just think, if we could share our thoughts with an experienced counselor, someone who knows the wider world—someone who won't laugh at the dreams of the young. But there's no such person in Miwa." Again he seated himself on the embankment, cross-legged, propping his elbows on his knees and cupping his chin thoughtfully in his palms.

"You've given me an idea, Jiro!" Now Gonsuke jumped up and started pacing about. "I think I know just the man. Have you heard of Hideyoshi?"

"Hideyoshi. Isn't he lord of Nagahama?"

"Indeed, he's one of Nobunaga's chief samurai. But he was born just leagues from here in Nakamura, a peasant like us."

Warming to his own words, Gonsuke quickened his pace. "My grandfather knew his father. Everyone says that despite Hideyoshi's high rank, he always offers a cheerful greeting and a kind word, even to the lowliest peasant."

Jiro sprang to his feet again. "I like what you're suggesting, Gonsuke! Maybe we could learn from this Hideyoshi. Suppose we seek him out and ask how he achieved his prosperity."

"My thoughts exactly." Gonsuke nodded, and Jiro could see a glimmering new resolve in his friend's eyes. "We'll finish planting by sundown. A trip to Nagahama takes a day and a half. By the Buddha, let's leave at first light!"

旅 2

The Road to Nagahama

The following morning found Jiro and Gonsuke far along the muddy road leading to the city of Nagahama, Hideyoshi's domain.

Though peace prevailed during the seasons of rice planting and harvest, Japan had been in turmoil for more than a hundred years. The troubles had started with the Onin War of 1467, in which the *shogun's* central government was toppled and the capital, Kyoto, reduced to a shambles. Since then, the *shogun* had been nothing more than a symbol, "an empty suit of armor," as Gonsuke often put it. Lawlessness spread through the land, rogues and thieves roamed freely, and provincial clans began to battle each other for territory. No longer a single nation, Japan had become a collection of sixty-six kingdoms, each ruled by a different warlord.

Among these was a minor baron, Oda Nobunaga, who planned to conquer every fiefdom and reunite Japan under a single sword. Ultimately, he would fail to realize that ambition, but Japan would be forever changed by his favored vassal, Hideyoshi—whose counsel Jiro and Gonsuke now sought.

Having walked six long hours, the travelers' aching legs and backs called for respite, and the midday heat soon parched their throats. Now they came upon a small farm and decided to stop for a short rest and a drink of water. An old stooped woman swept the dirt walk in front of her home with a broom.

"Good morning, Grandmother," Gonsuke called out. "Might we trouble you for some water?"

The old lady brightened at the unexpected company. "You and your young friend are welcome to rest your heels."

So Jiro and Gonsuke settled themselves on the ground in the shade of a small cherry tree as their host shuffled toward the farmhouse. Like every aged peasant woman, her crooked back kept her in the posture of a deep bow, testimony to a lifetime of sowing, planting, weeding, and harvesting. Watching her, Jiro imagined his beautiful young Shizue fifty years from now, and shivered despite the sun's warmth.

"You're most kind," said Gonsuke when the woman returned bearing two bamboo cups of water. The travelers drank deeply.

"Off to Nagahama, I reckon? What takes ye to the castle town today?" The old lady appeared eager for conversation.

"We have ... well, business with Sir Hideyoshi," said Jiro.

"Hideyoshi!" she exclaimed. "A grand samurai,

indeed."

"So we understand, though we haven't yet met him."

"A giant of a man," the woman enthused, her gaze turning glassy with awe. "Stands two heads taller than most samurai. Strong as a bear and wily as a fox. Why, at age twenty-one he bested the spearmaster Mondo in their first bout, though he'd never touched a spear in his life!"

Gonsuke and Jiro smiled, cheered to encounter one who could tell them more about the samurai they sought. They sat up straighter as she continued.

"After that terrible typhoon some years back, Hideyoshi repaired the Kiyosu Castle wall in barely a day. And in the battle of Okehazama he took fifteen heads—all with his short sword. Who do you think they found among the slain? The dreaded Haigo, man-monster of Mikawa!"

The travelers' eyes widened at the fearsome but unfamiliar name—and at the thought of those rolling heads. The old woman leaned closer with a conspiratorial whisper. "Hideyoshi's got magic powers, you know."

And now she began relating story after mythic story about Hideyoshi's amazing feats, her gaiety mounting as she spoke. Soon Jiro and Gonsuke glanced doubtfully at each other, wondering if this woman had confused the samurai with a figure from a fairy tale.

"Hideyoshi built Sunomata Fortress overnight. All the while, enemy arrows fell around him like rain!

Not a single shaft so much as pricked his skin! Then he swayed the warmaster Hanbei's allegiance away from Dosan—that dastardly Viper of Mino—to our good Lord Nobunaga. Together, Hanbei and Hideyoshi conjured a secret passage into Inabayama Castle, which Nobunaga soon conquered."

Abruptly Gonsuke rose and made an elaborate bow. "We'd best be on our way, Grandmother. Many thanks for your hospitality."

And with that the two friends took their leave amid the protests of their talkative host.

Jiro was laughing as they started again down the road to Nagahama. "When we meet Sir Hideyoshi we'd best beware his magic. He might turn us into a couple of sheep!"

Gonsuke smiled. "Some peasants believe everything they hear. Many still say forest yams become snakes when left in water too long." Then he grew pensive. "But who knows, there could be truth to the old woman's words. Maybe some sort of supernatural power underlies the prosperity of great men."

Jiro shook his head. "Only Hideyoshi himself can divulge his secrets. I can hardly believe everything our good grandmama had to say about him."

The two friends chuckled as they trudged along. At length they fell silent, each stunned in his weary condition by the beauty of the bright spring day.

When dusk descended they took shelter in a deserted temple, for bandits still prowled the countryside by night. At daybreak the two friends resumed their trek. After a five-hour walk the lush countryside fell away and dwellings became more frequent. Passersby began to appear in greater numbers, and presently the travelers found themselves on the outskirts of Nagahama.

Small homes doubling as shops opened directly onto the street, the unfastened slats of their roofs weathered gray and weighed down with heavy stones. Jiro and Gonsuke passed a seller of stoves, a rice merchant, and a stonemason's shop where workmen's hammers rang at chisels and newly carved lions stood guard with ferocious snarls. Fragrant smoke drifted from a *gyoza*-maker's stall, causing the travelers' empty stomachs to tighten with hunger.

The midmorning traffic thickened. Soon the two peasants shared the thoroughfare with other travelers: country-folk on their way to market; an itinerant oil peddler with his burden of heavy buckets suspended from a yoke across his shoulders. A group of noisy, grime-faced carpenters sauntered by bearing adzes and mallets. A fan seller stood at a corner hawking his wares in a shrill song, his colorful goods arrayed on a pole. Novice priests, clad in black jackets and white robes, carried begging bowls here and there.

The peasants, their gazes roaming about, swayed dizzily into each other as they navigated the swarm.

Occasionally an unemployed samurai wandered

past. Gonsuke and Jiro admired the fine figures these *ronin* cut, and how their *kimono*, though beaten with wear, hung clean and well patched on their taut frames. The two peasants felt safe—even protected—in the presence of such men. But other less reputable *ronin* slunk along the road as well, and the stale smell of last night's *sake* wafted from their sleep-rumpled garments. The two Miwa friends gave these unkempt rowdies wide berth.

At a wayside teashop Gonsuke suggested they rest briefly, and see what more they could learn about Hideyoshi. Poking their heads under a *noren* curtain, the peasants hailed the shop's proprietor, careful to stay outside the premises, for they couldn't spare the single copper coin required of every customer who entered.

A fat, jovial man waved from the dim rear of the establishment. "Come in, come in!"

Business was slow on this day, the only other patron being a gray-haired man seated on the shop's floor, sipping green tea. He looked up when Jiro and Gonsuke entered.

"Have some cool water—on the house!" bellowed the proprietor, bustling forward to set two earthenware cups on the table before the travelers, who accepted with thanks.

"No trouble at all. For payment I only ask ye to spread the word that Benjiro is a generous man! What brings ye to Nagahama today?"

"We're on our way to see Sir Hideyoshi," Gonsuke replied, trying to muster confidence in his words.

"Hideyoshi!" came the voice of the old man from his place across the *tatami* mat floor. "What business have you with that sly devil?"

The peasants turned, surprised.

The old man barked again. "Well? Do you know the rogue or don't you?"

Benjiro leaned close, murmuring, "Don't let old Shin intimidate you. He's surly but harmless."

"You seem to know more about Sir Hideyoshi than we," said Jiro to the old man.

"Know him? Why, he came to my textile shop as a fifteen-year-old runaway, looking to become a needle peddler. I lived in Kiyosu Town then." Old Shin threw back the remaining tea in his cup, then signaled Benjiro for a refill.

"Sir Hideyoshi bought needles from you?" said Gonsuke.

"He was no 'sir' in those days. Just a wretched little urchin—but the biggest trickster I ever met. He could talk a donkey owner into buying manure!" Shin slapped the tabletop and his empty cup rattled. "When Hideyoshi left Kiyosu he wandered from province to province, no better than a beggar. Somehow he apprenticed himself to the Matsushita, only to get fired for stealing. So he came slinking back to Kiyosu and sweet-talked Lord Nobunaga into hiring him."

Jiro's face fell. "But surely Sir Hideyoshi's a man of ability. Didn't he rebuild the Kiyosu Castle wall with amazing speed?"

"Ha! He and four hundred workers bribed with cash! That scrawny weakling could hardly lift a saw!"

The peasants swapped anxious glances.

"Scrawny?" Gonsuke said, uncertainty trembling in the word. "But as we understand, Sir Hideyoshi is tall and robust—and a hale warrior."

"Hideyoshi's a runt," sneered Shin. "Stands barely five feet tall. Couldn't skewer a drunken *ronin* with a nine-foot spear."

Now the two travelers from Miwa were thoroughly confused. Despite his caustic words, this old fellow seemed a more reliable witness than the gossipy grandmama whose home they had left the previous day.

"But Sir Hideyoshi distinguished himself at the battle of Okehazama," protested Jiro. "And what about his boldness in building Sunomata Fortress?"

The old man wagged his head as though chagrined to hear such foolishness. "Hideyoshi was a footsoldier at Okehazama. He just ran in after the real samurai had done the hard work demolishing Yoshimoto's camp. And building Sunomata? Why, Hideyoshi bribed Koroku's bandit gang to do the labor for him."

At the front of the shop the *noren* curtain parted as three new customers entered from the busy street. Eyeing the trio, Shin slammed his cup to the table, shouting, "Benjiro, you serve the best tea in Nagahama!" He wiped his mouth on his sleeve and turned back to Jiro and Gonsuke. His eyes narrowed. "You'd best be careful in any dealings with Hideyoshi. He's a sly one." And with that, he ducked under the curtain and disappeared.

Gonsuke and Jiro stared at each other, discouragement heavy on their brows. The long journey to this noisy city, only to hear conflicting accounts of their hero, had dampened their spirits. Should they have stayed in Miwa? Had they walked two days for nothing? After a moment, Gonsuke asked what both were wondering. "Master Benjiro, is there a temple close by?"

The proprietor told them the way to nearby Soganji. The travelers thanked him, left the teashop, and merged with the pedestrians thronging the road. They walked without speaking until they found the temple, then seated themselves on its grassy commons, relieved by the privacy and quiet. Here they contemplated the events of the trip so far.

Presently a little man approached from the raked stone gardens, turning a mischievous, wizened face to the lounging peasants. As he drew closer, they noticed that he wore the sturdy cotton robes of a samurai, but carried no swords. Behind this little figure stalked a bear-like warrior. At the sight of the peasants, the bear's left forearm came up to rest on the hilt of his blade.

"Good afternoon!" boomed the small man, in a powerful voice that would have seemed more natural coming from his gigantic counterpart. He was smiling warmly.

Jiro and Gonsuke returned his greeting, though with little enthusiasm.

The man stopped to appraise them. "Well now! If I were still as young as you two, I'd be more excited about life on such a beautiful day." Gesturing toward the Buddhist temple, he sighed happily. "I lived at a temple like this as a young boy. Life was harsh for me then, but these lovely grounds conjure pleasant recollections of that place. Ah, the magic of time and memory!" He threw back his head and drank in the sweet spring air.

The stranger's hulking companion stood motionless nearby, arms folded.

"Enough reminiscing," said the little man, as if to himself. "What brings you two to Soganji today?"

"A search for peace and quiet in a strange city," Jiro answered. "We've walked all the way from Miwa in hopes of meeting Sir Hideyoshi."

"Ho, ho!" the man said, his smile broadening. "Miwa and Hideyoshi: two names I know well. But you sound disappointed, my young friend. Have your hopes been dashed?"

Jiro studied the intriguing stranger who had instantly discerned his mood. The man looked older than his own father, at least fifty years of age. He had narrow, sloping shoulders, and stood a head shorter than Jiro, but his ramrod-straight posture gave him a mysterious air of authority. This stern quality was softened by dark, merry eyes that seemed capable of penetrating any object. Jiro decided he liked the queer-looking fellow, and spoke freely.

"Hideyoshi seems known to everyone, yet a different man to each. First we're told he's a giant and a master of martial arts, next we're to understand he's a clumsy midget. At mid-morning he's a hero, in the afternoon a coward!"

The stranger folded his hands before him. "What do you believe to be the truth?"

Jiro pursed his lips, thinking a moment. "Well ... perhaps Hideyoshi's character lies in the eye of the beholder. To a kind old woman who longs to see good in this world, he's a hero. To a bitter merchant, jealous of another's success, he's a trickster."

"Well said!" cried the little man. "People often see themselves in others. Tell me, why do you seek an audience with Hideyoshi?"

Now Gonsuke stood up and bowed respectfully. "We've come because we seek prosperity and fortune, as Sir Hideyoshi did. Perhaps a man who rose from the peasantry himself won't take offense at our simple-minded request for advice."

"Another answer well spoken! Most would prefer to wag their own tongues for an hour than listen for ten minutes to the advice of a genius." The stranger turned to his enormous companion. "Earthquake, what do you say we arrange for these fine fellows to meet with Hideyoshi? Then they can judge for themselves whether he's rascal or hero—or maybe a bit of both!"

From the big man's throat came a deep grunt of agreement, affirming the aptness of his nickname.

Jiro and Gonsuke bowed. "We're much obliged, sir!"

"We'll talk on the way to Nagahama Castle," said the little man.

The peasants smiled at one another in disbelief, then gathered their meager belongings and started toward the road with their benefactors. Though this stranger and his companion made an odd pair, clearly they were men of some influence.

"Is it true that Hideyoshi began his career as a needle peddler?" Gonsuke asked when the four had traversed the grounds and reached the main road.

"So the story goes," replied the little man. "They say he spent his whole inheritance—small as it was—on a quantity of needles, hoping to profit from growing demand for cotton clothes. But he lacked tradeskill, and an unscrupulous merchant overcharged him."

The eyes of the peasants met in surprise as both silently recalled their encounter at the teashop only an hour earlier.

"Some say Hideyoshi wandered the countryside selling his needles, at times below cost, until he was penniless. He slept rough, under bridges or on temple grounds, and resorted to taking odd jobs. Sometimes he went hungry for days.

"But by and by he made his way to Mikawa, home to the powerful Imagawa Clan, and managed to enter the service of a minor lord. There he began to fulfill his dream of working in a true samurai household. He distinguished himself quickly, and eventually went to work for Lord Nobunaga. He devoted himself wholeheartedly to his master's service."

"Is it true," asked Gonsuke, "that Hideyoshi rebuilt the Kiyosu Castle wall in only half a day?"

The small man laughed. "Apparently Hideyoshi likes to gratify his vanity by giving credence to exaggerated accounts of his deeds! The repair required a full three days, with ten teams of forty workers, all motivated by the promise of a bonus for speedy work."

"What about Hideyoshi's match against Mondo the spearmaster?" said Jiro. "We understand it was his first-ever bout with such a weapon."

This prompted another outburst of laughter, and again the two Miwa friends marveled that so small a body could house such a big voice.

"It happened this way, my friends. At a New Year's feast, Mondo, Lord Nobunaga's spear instructor, provoked a debate about tactics, claiming short spears were superior to long spears in battle. Hideyoshi, who lacked experience with spears of any type—long, short, or in-between—got dragged into the discussion. He considered Mondo a blowhard who only wanted to promote the views of his own school, so Hideyoshi wound up defending the use of long spears. Nobunaga commanded them to settle the issue with a contest between two teams: one armed with short spears, led by Mondo, and one with long spears, led by Hideyoshi.

"Mondo set to work relentlessly drilling his recruits in the finer points of close-quarters fighting. Hideyoshi merely trained his team to charge in unison. On the day of the match, Hideyoshi's men presented a wall of long staves that Mondo's team couldn't hope to penetrate with their shorter spears! Mondo was furious. He learned the hard way what Hideyoshi knew all along: technique alone can never overcome teamwork."

"What about Okehazama?" Jiro prompted. "We heard Sir Hideyoshi took fifteen heads during that battle."

Again the stranger laughed, and now a smile even crossed the dour face of the one called Earthquake.

"Fifteen! That would have surpassed Nobunaga's own achievement. Even if capable of such mayhem, Hideyoshi would hardly be so foolish as to outshine his employer in battle. In truth, at Okehazama it was all Hideyoshi could do to keep from falling off his horse!" The stranger guffawed as if savoring some private joke, and for the first time Earthquake chortled aloud.

"But surely Sir Hideyoshi is an accomplished samurai," Jiro said.

"My Miwa friends, on this point I can assure you: Hideyoshi is no fighter and never has been. I say so with authority, for I was present at Okehazama myself."

The two peasants stopped mid-stride.

"You were at Okehazama?" asked Gonsuke.

The stranger nodded, likewise drawing to a halt.

"But how could Sir Hideyoshi become a samurai," Jiro asked, "without knowing how to fight?"

"True samurai fight but rarely," intoned the little man, suddenly as solemn as a priest. Then he gave his listeners a whimsical wink. "And Hideyoshi never fights at all!" He sent himself into another fit of jollity and started walking again.

The young travelers traded perplexed glances as they followed.

"Hideyoshi distinguished himself," their host explained, "not through martial arts, but through devotion, hard work, gratitude, and service in non-military matters. And he had the wit to seek a powerful mentor in Lord Nobunaga. A man does well to choose his teacher carefully."

"Can you tell us about the building of Sunomata Fortress?" Gonsuke asked.

"Ah, yes," the little man replied. "One of Hideyoshi's most dangerous feats. Many believed that mission to be a death sentence. Two generals had already tried and failed to establish a fortress at Sunomata, losing many men in the attempt. It was a perilous spot, a crucial beachhead very close to enemy territory. But Nobunaga demanded a stronghold there, from which he could stage his invasion to defeat the Saito Clan at last. Hideyoshi conceived of the dangerous assignment as a challenging construction project that required the coordination of a huge number of workers."

"Was Koroku's bandit gang among them?" Gonsuke ventured.

The little man scowled for the first time since meeting the two peasants. The party of four now found itself at the gates of Nagahama Castle.

"Those who bow to no master are bandits in some eyes and free men in others. Hideyoshi trusts his very life to Koroku, from what I understand." He looked fondly toward his companion, towering nearby.

"On this point, in fact, I'm absolutely certain." Again a smile lit up his wrinkled face. "For I," he said, pausing impressively, "am Hideyoshi."

The Samurai's Secrets

*J*iro and Gonsuke stood for a moment with mouths agape, then together they fell to the ground in bows so low their foreheads brushed the earth.

"Forgive us, Sir Hideyoshi, for our unpardonable rudeness!" they cried.

"Nonsense." Hideyoshi motioned for the travelers to rise. "Most men ask for employment or favors. You two seek something more precious—wisdom. You'll be my guests. We'll take our midday meal together and I'll divulge what you long to know."

Hideyoshi waved his hand, and two guards standing by opened the Nagahama Castle gates.

"Go with Koroku," said the small samurai. "He'll show you where to wash up, then take you to my quarters."

The young peasants followed the giant across the castle grounds. In the courtyard a number of servants were passing back and forth in a brisk but hushed manner. Beyond the courtyard construction noise could be heard, and Jiro and Gonsuke saw teams of men at work hammering, raising walls, and splitting lumber. Farther out lay the brilliant blossoms of the castle gardens.

Koroku brought his followers to a servants' lodge, where they washed and made themselves presentable, all the while thanking the stars for their wondrous luck. Then Koroku led them across the way to the small wooden building that served as Hideyoshi's quarters. They were surprised at the modesty of the place. Aside from two hanging scrolls, a low table, and four *zabuton* cushions, the room was unadorned. Hideyoshi was already seated.

Servants brought a plain lunch of *miso* soup, pickled vegetables, and white rice, supplemented by one delicacy: broiled whitefish. At Hideyoshi's invitation, the two travelers fell upon the repast with gusto. Rarely had a meal tasted so good.

When they'd finished, another servant came to clear away the dishes on a red lacquer tray, and a full-bellied Gonsuke bowed yet again. "We're most grateful for your hospitality, Sir Hideyoshi. We must confess we were, well, surprised, to learn your true identity."

Jiro, too, bowed and nodded in agreement.

Their host suddenly looked serious. "You were amazed that the grand Hideyoshi is not a strapping, handsome samurai, but a wizened old midget who looks like a monkey!"

The Miwa friends reddened, for these had been their very thoughts. Hideyoshi's stern stare gripped them a moment longer, then he burst into laughter. "Don't be concerned, for I might have felt the same, were I you!"

Now the samurai rose, drawing himself up to his modest height, and with his tiny hands folded at his back began pacing the room. "Now, then. To the matter of the advice you seek. Your visit has prompted me to gather my thoughts. Though hardly old enough to be a sage, in four long decades I've experienced more than a hundred ordinary men will in a lifetime. And I've long believed that certain timeless principles underlie any honest man's good fortune."

Jiro and Gonsuke felt the ring of truth in the samurai's words. He spoke without a trace of boastfulness. They leaned forward to hear more.

"The secrets of fortune and fulfillment are as ancient as mankind itself. These secrets have always been known to the wise, but today, as in every age, only a few grasp their true meaning—let alone the awesome power such secrets unleash in the willing mind."

Hideyoshi stepped closer and spoke with ringing enunciation. "Comprehend the simple truths I shall reveal, and they will transform your lives as they did mine." Slowly, in his preternaturally loud voice, he uttered three words. *"Conceivable Means Achievable."*

The two visitors blinked. They gazed blankly at each other. "Conceivable means ... achievable?" Gonsuke repeated.

The young listeners jumped as Hideyoshi stamped an emphatic foot on the *tatami* mat floor. "Yes! That phrase is a key to your future, my friends!—a key to all good things in life!"

The samurai plopped down upon his cushion again. He raised his chin to Gonsuke. "Conceivable means achievable. What do these words mean to you, my peasant brother?"

Gonsuke swallowed. "That I am capable of accomplishing ... whatever I wish?" He raised a sheepish look to Hideyoshi.

Hideyoshi smiled. "If wishing were the way to achievement, good Gonsuke, then every beggar would ride a fine horse, and every nobleman would be a king. No, wishing will not make a thing so. Therein lies the difference between wishing and conceiving."

Again he jumped up and paced in long, thoughtful strides across the room.

"Conceiving, you see, means imagining that which is truly possible. Wish as I might, could I expect to outwrestle a man like Koroku, who boasts three times my weight and six times my strength? Preposterous! But it's perfectly conceivable that I might study and learn the art of *judo*, to successfully defend myself against a larger foe."

"What you say makes sense, Sir Hideyoshi," said Jiro. "But how is one to know what is truly possible for oneself, and what is not?"

"A fair question. Most men err not by overestimating their ability, but by underestimating their potential. To begin, then, the judgment of one's trusted friend may suffice. Here's an example. Jiro, to what occupation do you aspire?"

The young man's eyes shone. "Well, I'm a farmer, but more than the smell of budding rice plants, the fragrance of fresh sawn wood stirs my blood. You see, I feel most alive when building furniture or crafting adornments that might someday be hung in homes and temples. I long, Sir Hideyoshi, to devote myself to carpentry, but don't know how to realize my wish."

Hideyoshi turned. "Gonsuke, how do you appraise Jiro's skills as a carpenter?"

"The posts he carves rival the craftsmen of Ise. And the table he built for my wedding gift is as stout as it is beautiful."

Jiro beamed to hear his friend's praise, and Hideyoshi came around and placed his hands on the young man's broad shoulders. "You have the talent to be a carpenter, Jiro. And you have a clear goal. But understand what you lack: *a specific way of getting to your goal!* You must *conceive* of the path that will lead where you wish to go. Listen: Suppose you meet a wandering pair of strangers along the Great Eastern Sea Road. They hail you and ask for directions to a place you've never heard of. What's your first question?"

"I would ask if they knew some landmarks along the

way," Jiro answered. "Then I might be able to help."

"Exactly! And what if they replied, 'Just tell us the route'?"

"Why, they'd be a couple of asses," said Gonsuke. "Travelers without direction can't hope to get anywhere."

"Precisely my point," said Hideyoshi, and leaned close to emphasize each word with a shake of his finger. "For every stage of a journey, one must keep a clear end in mind. If you can conceive of the steps along the way to your destination, isn't it a straightforward matter to plot those steps and reach them one by one? Men fail less for lack of ability than for lack of clear intermediate goals.

"When you carved your table, Jiro, did it spring fully formed from the materials and tools at hand, without forethought?"

Jiro laughed. "Goodness, no! First I worked carefully to diagram the table with brush and paper."

"Indeed. You conceived the table in your mind, then on paper, before sawing the first piece of wood. Tell me, what can be accomplished that the mind has not first conceived?"

The two listeners shook their heads. "Nothing," they agreed.

"Precisely. But once the goal of your journey is fixed, it is simple to plot a course. There are many ways to travel from Nagahama to Kyoto. So a person looks at a map, chooses a route, then sets out for his first destination along the way."

"Can you give some examples from your own journey, Sir Hideyoshi?" asked Gonsuke.

Hideyoshi laughed. "That may take all afternoon. I do love to talk!"

The travelers chuckled and shifted their legs beneath the wooden table, keen to hear their new teacher begin his tale.

"Very well," said Hideyoshi, "I'll relate the story of my own first steps, which led me to acquire the secrets of prosperity."

He stood before them, gazing back into his memory.

"My family was poor, and my father died when I was only seven. Papa was a mere footsoldier in the army of Lord Nobuhide, but he considered himself a samurai. His military career ended when an arrow pierced his knee. As long as I can remember, he was crippled. Still, he regaled me nightly with colorful tales of his feats in battle—yarns that I now know were mostly imaginary. I doubt he ever rode a horse, but he meant the world to me."

Hideyoshi's eyes misted. It brought lumps to the throats of the two listeners to see their host overcome with such emotion, for they knew that in the world of the samurai, tears were considered unmanly. The peasants pulled their knees to their chests in rapt attention as though they, too, were small boys again.

"Father's death broke my heart. I'd always been a naughty lad, but now I became incorrigible. With Father gone, our family's poverty worsened, and Mother had no choice but to entrust me to the monks of Komyoji Temple. She hoped I would learn discipline there, along with rudimentary reading and writing.

"But it bored me to study lesson-books and recite sutras. I only wanted to be a samurai like Father, though the monks frowned on this desire. Soon I rebelled against that stifling temple life. I refused to complete my lessons. The monks promptly expelled me.

"Mother was at a loss. Hoping I'd learn a trade, she apprenticed me to one craftsman after another. The results were disastrous every time. How could I abide working anywhere but within a samurai household? The desire to follow the *Bushido* path burned within me, though I had barely the vaguest notion of how to realize this aim.

"At last came the day when I recognized my first step: I must strike out on my own. I must summon the bravery to leave Nakamura, my boyhood home! Yes, I resolved to journey to Suruga Province, ruled by the mighty Imagawa Clan. There I might work as a servant in the house of a great samurai. For the first time in my life, I had conceived of a clear and attainable objective. I was fifteen years old."

"You found a conceivable goal early," Jiro noted.

"Poverty was a blessing. Men not driven by necessity often take far longer to conceive a purpose in life. Though still a boy, I had already stumbled upon one secret of prosperity: *Conceivable Means Achievable.*"

Now the samurai paused from his tale to call for tea. A servant arrived and quickly poured a rich green infusion into a trio of cups. Hideyoshi dropped to his seat and stretched. The afternoon sunlight had started filtering through the slatted wooden windows. The two peasants watched the steam of the kettle coiling upward in the glowing rays. The servant withdrew, and for several minutes the threesome silently sipped the hot refreshment. Then Hideyoshi resumed.

"When I told Mother I was leaving home to seek service in a samurai household, she burst into tears. 'Hideyoshi,' she cried, 'you're a willful child. If your heart's set on becoming a samurai, I won't stop you.' She pried a loose board from the wall, reached behind, and extracted a burlap sack. 'I've been saving your father's inheritance for your coming-of-age day, but he would want you to have it now. Go, and may the goddess *Benten* bless you with luck on your way.'

"I hefted the sack, which bulged with copper coins. Never before had I held so much money, let alone imagined my poor parents could save such a sum. How they must have scrimped and sacrificed! For the first time in my short, selfish life, I felt truly grateful. My mind recounted all the pain I'd caused my mother, and I began to weep uncontrollably, a child knowing a parent's boundless love for the first time.

"'Dear Mother!' I cried. 'I'll make a name for myself and come back for you, just wait and see!'

"Staggering out of the wooden hovel that had been my intermittent home for fifteen years, I vowed I'd repay the debts owed my parents, the monks, and everyone who had tried to guide me straight along life's path. In that moment, you see, I came to understand that others had always served me. Now it was time for me to serve others.

"Hardships awaited, but my luck changed from that day, when I began to see that the very meaning of life lies not in being served, but in serving—and only a grateful soul can serve as one should."

Hideyoshi paused in an attitude like meditation. The two peasants sat unspeaking, watching as the slats of sun bathed the room around him in a golden hue.

By and by, the samurai broke the silence.

"My appreciative words and acts toward others begat favorable acts toward me. I soon came to believe that *Benten* herself was rewarding my thankfulness. I had arrived at another secret of prosperity: *Gratitude Attracts Luck*.

"My sack of coins presented a tempting target for roaming bandits, so I had quickly lightened the load. Hoping to increase my modest fortune, I'd purchased a quantity of needles to sell along my journey to Suruga Province. In those days cotton was increasingly popular for armor linings and civilian clothing, and I concluded needles would be in demand.

"Roving peddler that I now was, I saw many of life's transactions, commercial and social alike. I developed tradeskills and a sharp eye for assessing people. Of course, I still longed to become a samurai, but because I'd been ridiculed all my life for my puniness and lack of strength, I understood that wits and talent as a servant—not martial prowess—would win me entrance into a samurai house.

"By luck, opportunity came one day while I rested atop a bridge at Hamamatsu. I struck up a conversation with a passing samurai, and told him of my plans to travel to Suruga to join a household of the powerful Imagawa Clan.

"He scoffed. 'A needle peddler from Owari? They won't give you the time of day.'

"The remark raised my dander.

"'In that case,' I shot back, 'I'll have to put up with *you* as my new master!' At this the samurai seemed ready to strike my impudent head off, but then—a wonder—his scowl became a grin! He laughed and said he admired my spunk.

"His name was Naganori. He himself was a minor lord and vassal of the Imagawa. He allowed me to walk along with him, and as we walked I called him 'master' and told him what a faithful servant I would prove. He merely listened, seemingly amused at my presumptions. When we arrived at his modest castle, he announced to his household that he'd picked up a talking monkey on the road! It was, well, an endearment of sorts.

"Soon I found myself at work on Naganori's estate chopping wood, drawing water, feeding the horses, fetching tinder, and scrubbing floors, laboring harder than I'd ever labored in my life. I was grateful just to be in the service of a real samurai. Still, I continued to conceive of my greater goal, and looked for some way to distinguish myself.

"As a peddler I'd learned the market worth of goods and services. Samurai consider themselves above commercial matters, and I noticed they were often duped in business. I resolved to exercise my gifts on Naganori's behalf, and see that he was never shortchanged.

"My young friends, I tell you truly, it was knowing my own gifts that turned the tide. Though hardly a warrior, I had talents of organization, administration, and diplomacy. Soon I was purchasing supplies for Naganori's household, and not only improving relations with local merchants, but getting better prices. How could I have hoped to win respect without harnessing and strengthening my abilities? I couldn't. I had struck upon another secret of prosperity: *Know Your Gift*.

"During this time, I discovered a further means of distinguishing myself: sheer hard labor. My philosophy was to strive twice as much as anyone around me, to devote myself body and soul to every task, no matter how trivial, and to do so promptly and with good cheer.

"Some men see work as onerous, and fancy that their employers are obligated to furnish them with a living. The very opposite is true! In private, these same men disparage rather than praise their masters. Beware such ungrateful souls, for they are untrustworthy. I say that if you're going to work for a man, then work!"

Now Hideyoshi rose to his feet and shuffled to the western window. He slid back a panel to let in the cool air, which was growing soft and purple with twilight. The breeze ruffled the wisps of gray hair at the sides of his head. He looked out upon the castle garden a moment, breathing a deep, satisfied sigh.

"I'm no fighter, my friends," he continued, "but I'm a worker. No one outshines me when it comes to pure effort. And when I say 'effort', I mean breaking a real sweat!"

This last phrase seemed to inject the small samurai with energy, for he danced a brief, peculiar jig as he uttered it.

Jiro and Gonsuke smiled. This Hideyoshi possessed an uncanny command of voice, a quickness of emotion, and a physical spryness that charmed listeners into silence. Neither peasant had ever witnessed such humor and unabashed humanity in a man of this station, for most samurai held themselves aloof from commoners.

Hideyoshi returned and sat down in front of them,

leaning forward and squinting as though seeking to judge how well these two could guard another of his precious secrets. He must have deemed them worthy, for he went on.

"Understand this: Mediocre effort produces mediocrity, good effort produces good results, but extraordinary effort produces the extraordinary. That, too, is an important secret of prosperity.

"Naganori noticed my effort and eventually put me in charge of the castle storeroom. Do you see what had happened? In less than three years I'd worked my way from the most menial position to a manager of other servants. Make no mistake, it required extraordinary effort, but that effort produced extraordinary results!"

Again Hideyoshi sprang up, this time flinging out his arms and fairly shouting. "Look at the world around you! Tiny armies overpower far larger forces. A small *sumo* wrestler defeats his bigger opponent. And the rich trod our streets, surrounded by men of greater brilliance who remain penniless. What distinguishes those who succeed, I ask you?"

"Effort!" cried Gonsuke.

"Indeed, my peasant friend. *Effort Determines Results!*" The samurai performed another caper before dropping to his cushion again, happily exhausted by his story. He plucked a bean cake from the tea setting and nibbled thoughtfully.

In the momentary lull, Jiro and Gonsuke studied

their host. He looked immense and regal in his quietude, small and unhandsome though he was. And in that instant the peasants perceived that they were in the presence of a truly great man. Generations from now their children's grandchildren would tell the story of this day, when in front of the friends from Miwa Village this august but merry prankster had danced like a monkey while sharing his secrets. And now the peasants understood that even wise men are still men, and that the truly great, like Hideyoshi, remain plain and humble at heart.

Clapping his hands, the samurai called for evening tea.

When the three had refreshed themselves, Jiro asked why Hideyoshi had left Naganori's employment.

"Ah! An astute question, my good Jiro. And in the answer lies the essence of our final secret.

"My rapid rise within Naganori's household aroused the envy of the other servants. They feared being eclipsed by a newcomer—a small, ugly little peasant at that, let alone an outsider to the lord's family! I can't say their jealousy was completely unfounded, for I was proud of my accomplishments and had grown accustomed to giving orders, sometimes less than tactfully.

"Well, one day a cask of sweet potato liquor and a large quantity of candle wax went missing from the storeroom, and the other servants conspired to accuse me of stealing. I suspected they themselves had done the pilfering, but could furnish no proof. Lord Naganori called me to his chambers to confront the matter. I protested my innocence, and to my surprise, he believed me.

"'Hideyoshi,' he said, 'it must be difficult working among envious fellows. Perhaps a superior will always attract jealousy from those below. So be it, but bear this in mind: a leader must take care to share credit for successes, and must assist the less able in developing their own abilities.'

"'I will remember, Lord Naganori.'

"He looked me straight in the eye. 'You want to become a samurai, do you not?'

"I nodded vigorously.

"'Then I advise you to return home,' he said.

"This bewildered me greatly, I assure you. I begged my master to explain how dismissal would speed me on toward my goal.

"'You mustn't think of this as a dismissal, Hideyoshi,' Naganori replied. 'My fiefdom is too small to contain your ambition. You'll do well to enter the service of a lord destined for greatness. You should seek a position with Nobunaga.'

"'Nobunaga!' I cried. 'The wild one everybody calls Lord Fool?'

"'Nobunaga is no fool, Hideyoshi. Mark my words. Someday he may rule Japan.'

"I had nothing to guarantee Naganori's prediction,

but I had sense enough to take the advice of an older, wiser benefactor—one who held my best interests at heart. Before we parted, Naganori gave me a sack of copper coins in recognition of my service. I promised myself that I would repay this—yet another tremendous debt. Then I set forth on the long walk back to my birthplace—and home of Lord Nobunaga, the rising young warlord of Owari Province.

"A childhood friend of mine was now among Nobunaga's growing staff of servants. Thanks to him I secured a position as stablehand. With more than two years experience as a domestic, I was qualified for better employment, but I resolved to be grateful. However much this work might resemble a backward step, it was truly an opportunity. I strove to achieve a harmonious rapport with my colleagues in the stables. At the same time, as ever, I looked for a chance to distinguish myself. Luck soon swung my way.

"Lord Nobunaga was fond of hawk-hunting, and along with his senior vassals, three favored servants usually attended his expeditions. One day I managed to talk my way into replacing one of my colleagues on the lord's outing. Our party headed into the forest near Kiyosu Castle, led by Nobunaga himself, tall and eminent astride his steed.

"Our master's favorite hawk was always tied to its wooden perch by a cord of crimson silk. On this particular outing, a careless handler neglected to fasten the leash securely, and the hawk chased a sparrow into a chestnut tree. The hawk's cord became entangled in the branches, and suddenly the raptor itself was dangerously entwined. It hung upside-down by its tethered leg, beating its wings against the leaves as it tried to right itself.

"Lord Nobunaga shouted for assistance, but his vassals dithered, at a loss for action. Well, in my smallness I had always been a spry climber. So I broke from my place amongst the servants and scampered up the tree. I managed to calm the hawk and untangle it. Then I shinnied back down and presented her to my master with a deep bow.

"'Well done!' said Nobunaga, cocking his head to assess me. 'You're a new face here.' He looked closer, raised his eyebrows, then turned and addressed the entire entourage. 'One face in a million, at that!'

"There was a roar of laughter. But I had been ridiculed many a time on account of my looks, so when the laughter subsided I announced: 'They call me Monkey.' Then I added, 'Not merely because of my ugliness—which is unrivaled in Owari, if not all Japan—but because I make quick work of any task.' I bowed with all the formality I could muster, which was little given my meager experience addressing high-ranking samurai. 'I would be honored if your Lordship, too, would use this nickname.'

"Nobunaga prompted another round of mirth when

he announced, 'It looks like we've bagged a monkey today as well!' This time I laughed along with the rest of the party.

"That very afternoon the lord appointed me his personal sandal bearer. I felt like a child of fortune.

"Life had changed yet again. Now I directly served a highborn samurai who would become a mentor—and someone who would transform my destiny more profoundly than I could ever have imagined.

"As the days passed, my gratitude, devotion, and constant effort on Nobunaga's behalf won me his trust. Soon he confided his ambition to unify our ravaged nation under a single sword. Naganori had been right! Nobunaga was a genius, and my life's path had merged with a far greater purpose.

"Before long I rose to become Nobunaga's personal attendant, one of his most trusted vassals. The last secret of prosperity came from him. 'Monkey,' he would say, 'no man can succeed alone. Everything I've accomplished owes to capable vassals and partners like Shibata, Maeda, Niwa, Tokugawa, and you.'

"It thrilled me beyond measure to be mentioned in the same breath as Nobunaga's great generals and allies, and I took his message to heart, recognizing a precious fifth secret: *Collaboration Breeds Success.*

"The job of repairing the Kiyosu Castle wall tested my understanding of this secret. Typhoon winds had destroyed a long section of the wall, just as Imagawa troops were rumored to be preparing for an advance into Owari. The gaping breach invited disaster, yet the crew effecting repairs made slow progress. Spies, it turned out, had bribed the foreman to delay the work while the Imagawa forces drew nearer.

"Nobunaga banished the traitorous foreman, who was lucky to escape with his life. But now the repairs had to be finished quickly—before the Imagawa army could reach Owari's border. I saw that the intentionally poor direction had demoralized the laborers, so I proposed creating and explaining a new reconstruction plan, and offering a bonus for quick completion. To my surprise, Nobunaga put me in charge of the entire project and its four hundred workers!

"Now, instead of merely thrilling to the words of the Fifth Secret, I would have to heed it in action. I spent a sleepless night developing a plan, then addressed the workmen the following day.

"'You've labored long and hard under an untrustworthy foreman,' I shouted. 'But I'm here to tell you why your work on this wall is so important. Even as I speak, Imagawa soldiers march closer to our beloved home. Were they to arrive today, we would be overrun!'

"A troubled murmur rippled through the assembled workers.

"'Heed my instruction,' I continued, 'and you need not fear. Teamwork will be the key to saving ourselves and this castle! We'll divide into ten groups of forty men each. The first team to satisfactorily complete its section wins a bonus of fifty coppers per man!'

"Cheers went up. For the first time now, the men linked their toil to a greater goal. Beginning that day, they put their backs into their labor as never before. I happily pitched in, and was soon as mud-caked and grime-faced as any of them. At night, I celebrated the progress together with the workers, toasting them with cold cups of *sake,* and within three days we had completed the monumental task. Great feats are never accomplished without high spirits, and our joyful collaboration had bred success!"

Now Hideyoshi fell silent, subjected to Jiro and Gonsuke's admiring gazes. Dusk was drawing down in the castle grounds. Crickets had begun to chirrup.

"My young friends," said the samurai with a smile. "You're staring at me as if I had the power to save your lives."

He chuckled, and the trance of the peasants was broken. They both grinned in embarrassment. Jiro spoke up.

"Forgive us, Sir Hideyoshi, but surely you see how brilliantly you've spoken. And we've heard you right well. Our fortune is great today, to have met the likes of you."

"Ah, but am I really that different from you, my good Jiro? Or you, Gonsuke? We come from the same countryside, don't we? We all began as peasants, didn't we?"

"Indeed," said Jiro, "and this is what causes us wonder. You've achieved, Sir Hideyoshi, what no peasant-born soul has ever achieved in Japan. And surely those who heed the wisdom of your tale can realize their own smaller dreams. Gonsuke and I won't forget your Five Secrets of prosperity. Our lives will change after this day. Aren't I right, Gonsuke?"

"Jiro puts it exactly as I would, Sir Hideyoshi. Why can't I become the merchant I wish to be? I see now that there's nothing to hold me back!"

"Nothing at all," said Hideyoshi. "But remember, my friends, prosperity is as aptly measured in love, friendship, and personal fulfillment as in gold or fame."

"You speak the truth, Sir Hideyoshi," said Jiro. "And I believe I'll be most fulfilled as a carpenter."

Then something seemed to give the young man pause, and he fell quiet.

Gonsuke saw his friend's dismay. "What is it, Jiro?"

"Sir Hideyoshi's words have moved me beyond imagining," said Jiro softly. "But I fear that once we've returned home his words will remain just that—words—and back in our old Miwa habits we'll lose the will to act."

"What in Miwa holds you back?" asked Hideyoshi.

Jiro blushed. "There's a girl … "

"Say no more, say no more!" Hideyoshi grinned. "What's her name?"

"Shizue."

"Is she beautiful?"

"She outshines the sun. But I fear she may not ... "

Hideyoshi leapt up before Jiro could finish. "Jiro, when faced with a choice between following your dreams or giving in to your fears, follow your dreams! If this Shizue is a true woman, she'll choose a man who boldly pursues his destiny."

At these words, the young peasant released a deep breath and smiled.

But now a shadow passed over Hideyoshi's face. A grave and unexpected idea seemed to visit him. "However," the samurai said quietly, "we mustn't forget that a man's dreams can soon become obsessions. For I've seen how ambition can cloud a leader's judgment, my friends. In seeking prosperity, then, we must guard ourselves from impure motives, and strive to act with courage and character, honor and honesty."

With bated breath, the peasants harkened to the master's words.

"If only others," said Gonsuke, "could hear you speak, Sir Hideyoshi. It seems to me your secrets have the power to change Japan."

At this, an approving rumble came from the samurai's throat. His bushy eyebrows rose, and his eyes shone bright in the darkening room. "I believe you've hit upon something, Gonsuke!"

"Sir?"

"Who amongst the people of our divided nation

doesn't wish to better himself? Who amongst them doesn't long for such opportunities as I have seized?"

Suddenly Hideyoshi was up and dancing his sprightly jig again. "I was small, I was a peasant, I was born to the selfsame Japan as every commoner before me. I was even expelled from temple school! But by acquiring five simple secrets I created opportunity and changed my destiny. Why should the destiny of Japan be any different? She's at odds with herself, is she not? But this country can fulfill her destiny as I have mine!"

With ferocious energy he clapped his hands. The sound rang like a thunderclap in the room.

"What a great, great nation she could be! Oh, we are at the start of something, my young friends. You've helped me see it! I sensed there was a reason we met today. Here's what I want you to do … "

And Jiro and Gonsuke craned forward to listen as Hideyoshi instructed them to spread a message through all the villages roundabout: the master of Nagahama was founding a temple school. Any and all who desired to learn the secrets of prosperity, any and all who sought fulfillment in their work and brighter destinies, should gather at Soganji Temple in two weeks' time. It would be the beginning of a new Japan.

Two days later, the Miwa peasants had carried the news back to their village, after which it quickly traveled throughout the surrounding provinces.

Back home again, Jiro and Gonsuke found their spirits so greatly stirred that even at the close of each long workday, they could hardly sleep. Their imaginations whirred ceaselessly. As clearly as a watchman beholds a signal fire at night, each peasant now perceived his goals. It seemed that the counsel of the little samurai had started to make them both into new men.

Hideyoshi's public teaching would begin a fortnight hence, but Jiro and Gonsuke had already absorbed the samurai's secrets. In spirit, they were peasants no longer. And now, they said to themselves, to put the Five Secrets into action!

Hideyoshi's Five Secrets

1. *Gratitude Attracts Luck*
2. *Know Your Gift*
3. *Conceivable Means Achievable*
4. *Effort Determines Results*
5. *Collaboration Breeds Success*

The Temple School

One bright June morning along the road into Miwa Village a lean muscular figure shuffled through the heat and mud. He wore the garb of a samurai, but his clothes were disheveled and his long black hair had fallen unkempt over his ears. He sweated profusely in the early heat and made no effort to wipe his cheeks and brow, so that tracks of perspiration ran across his dirty face.

Villagers in the outlying rice fields stood to watch this *ronin* pass, then looked wordlessly at one another, shaking their heads at the sound of the stranger's fierce mutterings. Though alone, the man seemed absorbed in argument with some invisible and ill-intentioned companion.

Daizen—for that was the *ronin's* name—paid his observers little heed. He was too troubled to give a thought to his rough appearance. So deep was his distraction, in fact, that since leaving Inazawa late the previous night his sword had dragged in the dirt behind him. This would have shocked those who knew the *ronin,* for all were well acquainted with the great pride he took in his weapon. It was Daizen's habit to speak at length of the sword's origins.

"A genuine Kanemitsu it is," he would say, "given me by my first teacher."

And he would boast that the sword had passed the legendary test: when stood in the bed of a shallow brook, its edge facing upstream, it had cleanly sliced the leaves that floated down-current. Many a time Daizen had been goaded to sell the blade, but always he'd staunchly refused. Even offers of astounding sums failed to tempt him. "How could I trade my very soul?" he would say.

Now Daizen stopped beneath an enormous willow tree and used his sleeve to dab the sweat from his face. Looking back along the road, he noticed with despair the snaking trail his sword had carved. To think, he said to himself, that a once-proud samurai could soil his honor thus!

At that moment two peasants came loping past from the opposite direction. They moved with a sprightly, light-hearted manner that the *ronin* could only envy, heavy of spirit as he was. He watched them pass into the sunlight on the other side of the tree.

Happy bumpkins, he thought, and winced at his own misfortune—the frightful amount of money he'd lost gambling the previous night. Ill luck had reduced him at last to vagrancy.

I've as little to my name as those rustics, Daizen

told himself. Yet they seem carefree! And suddenly he was overcome by a peculiar desire to learn the nature of the peasants' happiness.

So the *ronin* found himself calling out to the retreating figures: "Friends, friends! Turn back a moment! Pause in the shade and tell me where you're bound in such good spirits!"

The two drew to a halt. For a moment they stood looking back at the rumpled *ronin* and conferring quietly. Then they turned and trotted toward the willow.

The smaller peasant carried a water gourd on a string. He unslung it from his shoulder, offering a drink.

"Much appreciated!" cried Daizen. He threw back his head and gulped with fervor while the peasants stood watching. When he'd slaked his thirst, he returned the gourd and said, "My friends, were I the moneyed man I was just last night, I'd thank you with coins, not mere words."

"We're glad to share our water, sir," said the smaller peasant. He had a wide handsome face, and a dark birthmark just below his left eye, which somehow gave him a distinguished look. "I'm Gonsuke, and this is my friend Jiro."

"And where are you headed today, Jiro and Gonsuke?"

"We're going to Nagahama," said Gonsuke, "to see Lord Hideyoshi."

"Well, is that so?" said the *ronin*, with feigned

gravity. He could only laugh at the notion of two crudely dressed farmers heading off to meet so famous a samurai. He looked the peasants up and down. The second one was younger—seventeen or eighteen perhaps—but broad-shouldered and stout. "Tell me, how do you expect to win an audience with Hideyoshi?"

"We met him last month," blurted Jiro. "And he invited us back."

Daizen's jaw dropped. He couldn't hide his astonishment, for something in the bearing of the two rustics testified that they spoke the truth.

"How in the world did two ... er, fellows like you arrange a meeting with the Lord of Nagahama?"

"Like us, Sir Hideyoshi was born a peasant," said Gonsuke, "so we sought him out to ask his advice on how we might prosper as he has."

Daizen slapped his head twice in amazement—first at the simplemindedness of the two peasants' conception—and again because they had achieved their artless aim. He began to perceive that he was dealing with men who, despite their lower status, were somehow superior to himself, and were journeying toward a humble, yet profound destiny. This awareness grated against the *ronin's* damaged pride, but he sensed opportunity and adopted a conciliatory tone. "Well, now, that's a stupendous piece of luck, my friends. I wish some of your good fortune would rub off on me."

"You've had bad luck, sir?"

"The worst."

And now awkward moments dragged by as the *ronin* bemoaned the accursed wheel of fortune which had turned against his hopes.

Two years earlier, Daizen had been a trusted retainer and respected swordsman of the Takeda Clan. But after enemy gunners overwhelmed Takeda's mounted samurai at the battle of Nagashino, the *ronin* had found himself masterless and unemployed. He'd suffered much sadness at the death of his admired lord, and in his despondency had fallen to drinking and gambling. He survived by working as a mercenary and giving the odd fencing lesson, but his gambling losses mounted, and soon a gang he owed coerced him into enforcing the collection of others' debts at the point of a sword. What he didn't tell the peasants was that to win freedom—plus a few golden *ryo* in traveling expenses—he'd reluctantly committed a final, dastardly act on behalf of his underworld employer. The memory shamed his samurai spirit and had haunted him since.

Jiro and Gonsuke lowered their eyes as Daizen spoke, glancing sidelong at each other, nonplussed by the *ronin's* self-pitying display.

"Ah-ha!" Daizen interrupted himself. "I thought you averted your eyes in deference, but no, clearly you're stunned in admiration of my sword!"

This remark surprised the peasants, and Jiro stuttered, "Well ... it's a beautiful sword. You must be very proud of it."

"A genuine Kanemitsu! When stood in a stream, it slices the passing leaves. I've cherished it many years."

The *ronin* drew the blade and held it flat across his palms. The greenish tree-light glinted brilliantly off the steel, such that the peasants raised their hands to shield their eyes.

"But listen, my friends," said the *ronin*, his voice dropping to a crafty pitch. "Since you're off to Nagahama, why don't you ask whether Hideyoshi's interested in such a marvelous sword. There could be something in it for you both."

Jiro and Gonsuke shifted about, embarrassed on behalf of the *ronin*. "But sir," said Gonsuke, "we're going to Nagahama not to trade, but to hear Sir Hideyoshi's teachings."

The heedless *ronin's* voice took on a tone of desperation. "How much do you think Hideyoshi would pay? Forty *ryo*? Thirty?"

Gonsuke stepped forward and touched the *ronin's* sleeves. Softly he said, "Sir, please. We've never seen such a fine blade. Even if Sir Hideyoshi wanted your sword, it shouldn't be sold."

"Gonsuke's right," added Jiro. "You are a samurai. Please put the sword away and promise you'll never part with it."

Daizen stood stunned. He looked down at the sword in his hands, blinking his eyes, wonderstruck.

Strange, he thought, how these two should school me in honorable conduct. But so it is! In these tumultuous times the high and mighty may fall, and the low and humble may rise.

To the peasants it seemed that the *ronin* was awakening from a stupor. He slowly sheathed the sword and made a deep bow. "My forthright friends," he said, "I'm indebted to you."

The peasants blushed.

"You see," said Daizen, "bad luck has ... confused me so that, well—I seem to have forgotten myself. As if I've been walking in a dream." The *ronin* hung his head in shame.

"We understand," Jiro replied, glancing anxiously at Gonsuke. "Bad luck can distract anyone. That's why successful men like Sir Hideyoshi don't rely on luck but on other secrets."

"Other secrets?" said Daizen, looking up. "Like what?"

"Why don't you come with us to Nagahama? At the temple school, you can hear the answers from Sir Hideyoshi himself."

"Temple school?" said Daizen.

"Yes, come with us!" said Gonsuke, and he told the *ronin* of the enterprise the renowned samurai was starting, a historic gathering to which any man, regardless of his station in life, could come and learn the principles of prosperity and fulfillment.

Humbled by the dignity of the two peasants, and

intrigued by the chance to meet Hideyoshi, the *ronin* quickly agreed to accompany them. "By the way, I'm Daizen," he told them. "And it's my pleasure to meet you both."

As the threesome departed the shade of the willow and set out along the road to Nagahama, the *ronin* gathered his hair and smoothed his disheveled garments. Then he hitched up his belt and tightened it fast, so that his sword hung properly off the ground.

The farmers in the rice fields looked up again as Daizen passed with his two companions. The villagers noted a new straightness to the *ronin's* posture and a new grace in his step, and, for a brief moment before returning to their toil, wondered why he was going back to where he had come from less than an hour earlier.

Two days later in Nagahama, the June warmth was already thick by midmorning. The shady grounds of Soganji Temple, normally quiet on Sunday, buzzed with anticipation. Students had gathered from the provinces of Owari, Mino, Echizen, Iga, Ise, and beyond. They came from all walks of life: peasants, craftsmen, merchants, Portuguese traders, Japanese and Jesuit priests alike. Amidst this milling multitude the name "Hideyoshi" fluttered about like an elusive dragonfly.

By and by, the crowd converged on the crest of a

grassy mound just beyond the temple wall, settling into a semicircle around a large stump upon which the great Hideyoshi would preside. Expectations hung immense and palpable above the many heads.

Presently a hush descended and a tiny, dwarf-like man appeared amid the studentship, accompanied by a behemoth of a samurai. The little fellow and his huge companion walked straight to the center of the crowd where, pausing, the small one was seen to be scarcely taller than the stump. Thorny eyebrows accentuated the disproportionate enormity of his balding head with its thin gray strands of hair. He wore sandals and a simple white *happi*, the same coat worn by some of the workmen sitting before him.

Looking upon this curious figure, many of the students supposed him a vassal and wondered if Hideyoshi would not appear after all. Had the famous samurai sent these oddly paired servants to announce his absence?

With a fleet motion the tiny man leapt atop the stump and at once, by some mysterious power, assumed a great quality of assurance, a remarkable charisma that seemed to enlarge his stature. Suddenly he commanded not only attention but respect. His voice boomed forth.

The listeners drew themselves up in surprise, so much more impressive was the voice than anything the first sight of this man might have suggested. And the little man's face, the students now perceived, bespoke not lowliness or the worry that attends it.

Though homely indeed, the face betrayed a quiet, knowing mirth, as though the small fellow was privy to centuries, not mere decades, of human experience.

"When I was a boy of four," he declared, "a fortune-teller passing through my village looked into my eyes and told me I had two pupils in each. The crone said this characteristic foretold my future as a leader of men. I believe my fortune has increased today, for I stand here now and behold at least a hundred pupils. That's fifty more to each eye!"

Laughter quaked softly through the crowd. The small man stood smiling, watching the sunny faces. When silence again fell, he announced: "I am Hideyoshi."

This news was met by thunderous applause, and amidst the uproar voices rang out: "Lord Hideyoshi, tell us how you succeeded in building Sunomata Fortress!"

"Speak of your negotiations with Hanbei!"

"Tell how you halved fuel expenses at Kiyosu!"

"Your encounter with the Single-Minded Sect!"

"The Battle of Nagashino!"

The little teacher stood placidly with hands folded at his back. He murmured something to his hulking companion and the ogre withdrew. Then, with a graceful wave, Hideyoshi caused the noise to cease. In the breathless silence that followed, his wizened eyes caught sight of two young peasants at the rear. He gestured toward them. "I wish to thank my friends Jiro and Gonsuke for inspiring the idea of this temple school."

More applause followed. Jiro and Gonsuke grinned with embarrassment.

Hideyoshi raised his hands. "You all ought to know from the outset," he began, "that you've gathered today to hear the words of an uneducated man. As a boy, I neglected my studies and was rightly expelled from a temple school much like this one."

A chorus of chuckles rippled across the knoll.

"And let's be honest: Not only am I the most unlearned teacher in Nagahama, I'm also the ugliest!"

At this the students roared with delight. Voices in their midst murmured to one another:

"Unlike most samurai, to mock himself!"

"He doesn't begrudge talking to commoners!"

Hideyoshi continued, "Many prosperous people are far from handsome, even grotesque like me. I can't explain why. Maybe unsightly men become successful because they're used to working harder to attract women. Looking at your ugly mugs, I can see that you're all destined for greatness too!"

The students heaved with laughter again, slapping their sides and turning to guffaw with their neighbors.

The teacher waited for the merriment to subside, then spread his arms wide. "Welcome to our temple school, where any man, regardless of background, may study and learn the principles of fortune and fulfillment. I suspect that you've come to hear me disclose a secret—the secret of my rise in the world."

A murmur of eager consensus was heard. Hideyoshi paused, allowing an expectant silence to fall. When it seemed at last that the stillness would burst, he announced, "I fear I must tell you the truth. *There is no secret.*"

A dumbfounded surprise hung heavy in the air. Hideyoshi hopped down from the stump and began walking slowly around the assembled pupils, his sandaled feet perfectly tracing the semicircle. All watched as the little teacher's keen eyes coursed over the rows of students, seeming to absorb each person's every detail.

"No, there is no secret. But there are five eternal principles on which the ancients' prosperity was founded, principles which will continue to serve successful men long after our grandchildren's children have turned to dust."

Returning to the front row, Hideyoshi crouched with the energy of a panther ready to spring. In a beguiling whisper, as if preparing to unravel some supernatural puzzle, he declared, "Each of my five truths already lies concealed within your own minds. My task is merely to draw them out. To accomplish this, we will apply common sense to our own experiences."

The samurai mounted the speaking stump again. "Upon examination, you will find the five principles so simple and self-evident that you'll wonder why you needed an ugly monkey like me to help you recognize them."

Another chorus of laughter followed, during

which Hideyoshi seated himself atop the stump, perfectly erect, his eyes bearing down upon the students with quiet intensity. After a long moment he posed his first question: "Why are some men prosperous and others not?"

A hand shot up at the back of the assembly. It was the *ronin* Daizen, who eagerly introduced himself to the group. "Luck plays a part. Surely a person cannot attain success like yours without the blessings of luck."

"Indeed, and I do not disagree," Hideyoshi replied. "I have been as lucky as any other successful person. Daizen raises a subject worthy of discussion. Who among you would like to attract more good fortune?"

A tremendous huzzah erupted, every man crying out.

"Me!"

"I, too!"

"Yes, more good luck—and plenty of it!"

Hideyoshi smiled. "Well then, if prosperity results from luck, let's hear some examples of men who were visited by sheer luck and experienced—with no effort on their part—enduring fortune thereafter."

No one replied. Hideyoshi waited. The stony silence grew uncomfortable.

"Can no one think of a single instance?" said the teacher.

A plain-robed peasant rose to speak. "While picking mushrooms in the woods one day, I happened upon a bridled horse wandering riderless," he volunteered. "When I returned it to Inabayama Castle, I received a golden *ryo* as reward, for it was one of the master's favorites."

"Good luck indeed," said Hideyoshi. "Did you thereafter search the forest daily for riderless horses?"

The grinning peasant shook his head and sat down amid the affable chuckles of his classmates.

"Who else can relate an instance of luck?" asked the teacher.

Every student looked about, expecting a reply. None came.

"Then such luck must be rare indeed," said Hideyoshi. "The truth is this: Fate prefers no man over another when bestowing her random fortunes. Nor do such fortunes endure. That being so, where else might we look for luck?"

A young craftsman stood. "At the dice table," he suggested. "I admit I've tried my hand there once or twice."

"With what success?" a voice called out.

"None whatsoever," the young man replied with a sheepish grin. "The goddess *Benten* chose not to send luck my way."

He returned to his seat and exchanged friendly jostles with his neighbors.

"Another worthy subject!" Hideyoshi exclaimed. "Gambling troubles many men, for it's a common instinct to seek a quick profit with no effort by wagering. Who among us has succeeded at the gaming tables?"

Daizen spoke again. "I've won plenty," he declared with evident pride. "Once I acquired twenty golden *ryo* with a single throw of the dice!"

Sounds of wonder surged through the crowd. Twenty *ryo!* Many had never beheld, let alone possessed, such an enormous sum.

"Tell us, Daizen," said Hideyoshi, "did gambling bring you enduring prosperity?"

The *ronin's* face reddened. "If it had, I wouldn't be here today," he admitted, drawing sympathetic laughs from his listeners.

Now a Portuguese merchant rose at one side of the assembly and introduced himself as Fernao. Doffing his large and doughy hat, he began, "Forgive me if I speak not so correctly, for I am come to Japan for trade of goods from my home in Portugal. I wish to talk, Sir Hideyoshi, about gambling kind of man. This kind is many, many in Portugal."

Fernao made an embarrassed bow, apologized for his speech once more, and continued. He described a game he'd seen played in Lisbon and Oporto involving a box and a token. The bottom of the box was lined with a grid, he explained, and this grid was marked with a zero, a double zero, and the numerals one to ten. Players placed bets on where they believed a token would come to rest in the grid after the box was lidded and shaken. The operator promised to pay ten to one on any successful wager.

"I watch many man lose this game," said Fernao. "And how surprised was I, some time later, to sit in tavern where I hear the nearby talkings of the gambling owner. This man was much drinking when a fellow say to him, 'How does your house make winning at that game?'

"'Zero and double-zero are my great friends,' the owner say. 'Even if players bet one coin on every number, I get twelve coins but pay only ten. So I can't lose!' Like they say in Portugal fishing village: Man looking for success in gambling-house is like man looking for fish in tree. He never find it."

Hearty laughter resounded across the knoll.

"Few men understand," said Hideyoshi, "how certain is the gambling-house's profit, and how sure their own chances of losing. They continue to believe in random luck."

"But men sometimes win big, as Daizen did," a peasant called out.

"True enough," Hideyoshi replied. "But over time, no man can beat mathematics cleverly aligned against him. Since I first started serving Lord Nobunaga nearly a quarter century ago, I've dealt with thousands of men. Never have I met a single one who experienced steady success in gambling. Can anyone name such a man?"

No one replied. Finally, Fernao spoke again. "I know such man in Portugal. But he run the game, not play it!"

The knoll echoed with mirth again, and none enjoyed it more than the instructor, who paused for a sip of water from a stoneware cup. "We've seen that the goddess *Benten* bestows pure luck rarely and randomly, and that true fortune awaits no one at the gambling tables. How else might we seek to entice prosperity?"

"By our own talents and trades," said a burly craftsman. "A person increases his luck through his own efforts."

"True enough," said Hideyoshi. "Who can elaborate on this point?"

"Sir Hideyoshi!" cried an eager voice in the second row. All heads turned as a *tofu* maker rose to address the studentship. He was thin and small-shouldered and wore a big straw hat. "I'll tell a tale that shows how a man invites luck through hard work—and by welcoming opportunity."

At Hideyoshi's nod, the *tofu* maker removed his hat and bowed respectfully to his listeners. "My neighbor is a lacquerware craftsman by the name of Kichibei. For years I watched Kichibei slave at his art with little result, as buyers repeatedly passed him by to do business with a craftsman in the next village whose name had become associated with lacquerware of finest quality. My neighbor had no choice but to work every waking hour, toiling as a farmer by day and struggling to make lacquerware by night—just to keep his wife and children from going hungry. But I never heard Kichibei complain. He was always grateful for what little he and his family possessed. And he never ceased to labor at his craft, and to do so joyfully.

"Last year, Kichibei's lacquerware caught the eye of a retainer to Lord Kagekatsu as he was passing through our village. The vassal ordered twelve of my neighbor's bowls on behalf of his master, demanding that they be delivered within four day's time. Unable to afford assistants, Kichibei went without sleep for three nights that he might deliver the order in a timely manner, and that the bowls might glow with the finest luster. He succeeded in filling the order, and the excellence of his work pleased the vassal greatly.

"Because of this, Kichibei's reputation is growing and his lacquerware is coming to be recognized as a worthy rival to that of the man in the next village. Now my neighbor enjoys a robust business. He no longer tills a landlord's field; instead, he fills orders all day and enjoys rest at night.

"In Kichibei I've seen how one may till the soil of his own talent with unfailing devotion, so prosperity can grow therein. And then when opportunity called, my neighbor seized it with the sure hands of a practiced craftsman."

Fernao jumped to his feet. "This story very exciting. Opportunity, she come and go quick. Only man who is ready can grab her and make success."

"Indeed! *Benten* calls only upon those who prepare for her visit," added Hideyoshi.

"I'll tell a story," offered a middle-aged merchant, "that illustrates how opportunity knocks. When accepted, it becomes 'luck.' Ignored, it vanishes—to the regret of those like me, who fail to answer."

Hideyoshi nodded and the man stood to address the listeners.

"My father was a lumber merchant who enjoyed modest success. When illness forced him to retire, he entrusted the lumberyards to me. One day soon afterwards he called me to his side.

"'My son,' he began, 'I'm not long for this world. Before I go, hear the advice I failed to follow at your age. Had I done differently, our family's fortunes would be far greater today.'

"Father told me his friend's son was planning to lease a quarry that lay unused on a local landowner's property. The son, who kept a keen eye on current affairs, had noted the growing use of muskets manufactured in Tanegashima and Sakai. This observant young man concluded that warlords across Japan would eventually begin building their fortresses with stone rather than wood, to prevent them from being pierced by musket fire. He was convinced demand for stone blocks would soar, and that a quarry would become a valuable asset. He had a plan for a consortium of twelve local merchants to pool their funds and lease the quarry, sell stone, and share the earnings.

"'Listen to me, son,' my father said, gripping my shoulders with what strength remained in his failing hands. 'This is an opportunity to join an enterprise planned by wise and honest men, one offering good chances of success. Building materials must change with the times. I've been overly cautious, but you needn't repeat my mistakes. Seize this chance before it slips away!'

"Well, being young and unwise, I failed to recognize the opportunity in front of me. Ignoring my father's advice, I spent my time and money keeping the lumberyards stable and investing in inventory—more than was needed. And as the new head of the family, I wanted to enjoy some of the finer things in life. I spent my extra income refurbishing my home. In doing these things, I put off what action I might have taken on the quarry opportunity until it was too late. Within a few years, demand for stone soared, and the quarry had become the most profitable enterprise in my province. I had let a good venture pass me by. The lesson I learned is that 'good luck' really means taking advantage of opportunities."

"I've led many men," Hideyoshi interjected, "and sheer luck visited only a handful. But opportunity—in one form or another—called on each and every man at some point in his life. Yet only a few enthusiastically seized the day. Those who did so prospered."

Hideyoshi turned to the *ronin* who had accompanied Jiro and Gonsuke to the temple school. "Daizen, you suggested the topic of luck for our discussion. What do you say now?"

The *ronin* stood. "Until today," he said in a humble voice, "I viewed luck as something bestowed by the hand of Fate. Now I see that luck is self-made. It is attracted by devotion to one's own skills and effort, and won by accepting opportunity."

Hideyoshi smiled. "Daizen, you've stated well the truths we've discovered together. *Benten* is a fickle lady indeed, but she is successfully wooed by those who work hard and remain at the ready."

By now the morning had eased past noon into the rich, humid warmth of full day. Hideyoshi spread his hands and called for a respite.

"Let us gather again after a midday meal," he said, "and together we will explore the first, and perhaps most mysterious, of our five ancient secrets—a certain quality by which wise men have attracted luck for ages."

饮水思源 5

Gratitude Attracts Luck:
The Scroll of Fortune 🌿

"Who is the luckier man: He who rides in a fine palanquin, or he who carries the rider?"

All across the grassy grounds of Soganji Temple, the faces of eager listeners shone in the afternoon sun, and they answered readily as if in a single voice. "He who rides!"

At this the distinguished merchant Manzo smiled knowingly. He was a little man with a long mustache, the ends of which dangled well below his chin. He presided upon the speaking stump, having been invited by Sir Hideyoshi to address the pupils of the temple school.

"Many years ago when I rode such a fine palanquin," Manzo began, "I thought as you do. I believed luck belonged to he who is served. But after luxury had coddled my mind and softened my hands, I learned a greater truth: Good luck arises from serving others."

The humid summer air had thickened with the rising of the afternoon sun. Manzo waved a fan in one hand, and the ends of his thin mustache swayed like the fronds of a willow. On the fan's gold-speckled paper his listeners could see an exquisitely wrought Chinese maxim, inscribed with the red seal of the calligrapher.

"Sir Manzo," said a thin charcoal maker who had risen near the back, his weathered face stained by the black lines of his trade, "this morning we learned to attract luck by developing our talent and accepting opportunity. Now you say it is as servants that we will become lucky. Won't you reveal your meaning?"

"Indeed I will," replied Manzo. "Listen closely today, and my story will illustrate an ancient principle whose mysterious power no human mind can fully fathom. Yet its truth is as constant and unchanging as the sun."

The assembly rustled with anticipation as the venerable merchant settled back onto the stump to begin his tale.

"As a boy I always wore the finest garments, ate the finest foods, and took my leisure at the finest entertainments. Everything I wanted came to me without a minute of effort on my part. My father was a peasant, but in the chaotic aftermath of the Onin War he became a merchant and adopted the surname Kato. In his success he grew to be widely respected, treated much like a nobleman. As do many parents who come late to distinction, Father wished to spare his son the bitter hardships of his own youth. So I grew up as spoiled as a prince—a beloved only child who never longed for anything. But in truth I was deprived of something precious: the lessons of struggle, which reveal a man to himself.

"One day I was passing with my father's procession through Okazaki in Mikawa Province. I rode in a palanquin, customary for a pampered fifteen-year-old whose silken sandals rarely touched rough earth.

"As we crossed a bridge in the early hours, our procession halted and a commotion awoke me. I peeped through the curtain. Our attendants had surrounded a young lad who lay sleeping in the road.

"One attendant roused the boy with a vicious kick. 'Out of the way, you rude fellow! Can't you see Master Kato is coming through?'

"Rubbing sleep from his eyes, the boy stood. His face was fierce and defiant. 'Your master may ride in comfort while I lie in the dirt, but that doesn't give him, you, or anybody the right to treat me this way!'

"'Beggar! How dare you speak thus!' Steel glinted in the morning light as the attendant drew his blade.

"'Danjiro! Put that sword away.' Father's voice boomed across the bridge. He strode forth from behind my palanquin. 'What's going on here?'

"The angry attendant bowed. 'This vagrant was blocking the road, Master Kato.'

"Bristling, the urchin boldly addressed the circle of grown men surrounding him. 'You all show your ignorance by concluding that I'm a beggar because I lie here.

This bridge is not meant for you alone. It's intended for the community, so all who pass along should be careful to act politely to fellow travelers. To deal with someone lying in the road by kicking and calling him a beggar is dishonorable behavior, I must say.

"'But,' the boy continued with a sly smile, 'if you take me for a beggar, then make good on your judgment by giving me some food.'

"'Watch your tongue!' blustered Danjiro, purple with rage.

"'Now, now,' said my father, stepping closer for a look at this brazen boy. 'The lad's words make sense.' He knelt down and gazed into the young man's hungry eyes. 'I know how it feels to scrape the bottom of your rice chest.' Removing a string of copper coins from his purse, Father placed it into the boy's hands. 'Run along and buy yourself a square meal.'

"I'll never forget the glowing pride on that boy's face as my palanquin passed and our eyes briefly met. Those eyes of his seemed to say, 'Watch, my fine palanquin-boy. People often exchange places; the high become low, the poor, rich. Someday you may find yourself tying my sandals!'

"Spoiled as I was, I could only envy the youth's independent spirit, his resilience in the face of struggle—not to mention his great pluck in standing up to an entire entourage of privileged men! For years the scene lingered in my mind, and today you may see for yourselves to what heights that boy rose. For he is here among us, grown to illustrious manhood—and it's high time I tied his sandals!"

So saying, Manzo bent to the leather straps at Hideyoshi's feet.

Gasps echoed through the crowd. Could it be? Hideyoshi a beggar!

"Yes, friends," cried Manzo. "The boy on that bridge decades ago was none other than our esteemed Master Hideyoshi." With a wink he added, "That monkey face is emblazoned in my memory."

The tiny samurai was beaming with amusement. He waved his finger in mock scolding. "Manzo, today many a man could lose his head for comparing me to an ape. Fortunately, you're not among them."

Whereupon the two old friends embraced before the astonished listeners, who clamored with delight at their professors' antics.

Turning to the pupils, Hideyoshi raised his arms, palms upward as if drawing upon a higher power. "I stand before you as a man who once begged," he thundered, "and a man who is better for it. Listen well to Manzo's tale if you would learn the first secret of fortune and fulfillment: *Gratitude Attracts Luck.*"

Quiet descended and Manzo began to speak again in a sure, clear voice.

"Soon after that encounter at Okazaki my fortunes changed. My mother died. Father and I were grief stricken. But a year later Father married a widow with one son. She was a crafty woman of hard and selfish spirit—and a stunning beauty. By her charms she had wrung great sums of money out of more than a few rich men. Now she manipulated Father's affections in his state of enduring grief. From the start, stepmother hated me deeply and began plotting to position her own son as my father's successor.

"Father and stepmother had been married barely a year when Father's heart stopped beating during his sleep one summer night. Suddenly I was bereft of that gentle man who had shown me nothing but love my entire life. How blessed I had been while he lived, how assured of every earthly comfort. And now I was left alone with my stepmother and her mean-spirited son.

"The heartless woman no longer disguised her intentions to control my family's fortune. There was much discord between me and the schemer, and finally, on my seventeenth birthday, she told me that if I agreed to leave and never return she would see that I carried a load of golden *ryo* with me at my going, enough to live in luxury for a lifetime.

"Still heartbroken by Father's death, and too weak to resist this wretched temptation, I accepted the money.

"As I left the only home I'd ever known, I carried amongst my things a certain object my father had given me long before. When I was barely old enough to read, he had pressed an ancient yellowed scroll into my hands. He'd cherished this heirloom since his own youth, in the days when he first rose from a peasant birth to distinction as a merchant. The scroll bore, in bold and jagged calligraphy, the words of an ancient Chinese proverb:

> *When you drink from a stream,
> remember the spring*

"'This scroll is priceless,' Father told me, 'but only to the man who truly grasps its message. The greater your understanding, the greater its value. Keep the scroll always, for he who holds to its wisdom becomes pure of heart, a willing servant, and the richest of men.'

"I read the words of the scroll that day, but they made little sense to my young mind. *When you drink from a stream, remember the spring.* What could such a saying possibly mean? And how would it make me a rich man, as Father promised? Anyway, I was already more wealthy than every other boy I knew. I put the scroll away and forgot it entirely, until the day I accepted stepmother's bribe and gathered my things, the scroll among them. Its ancient message was mysterious as ever. Nevertheless, I carried the heirloom with me as I set out upon the road.

"At first it hardly appeared to matter that I had surrendered my rightful place as Father's successor, for life seemed only to improve. Indeed, I congratulated myself for accepting my stepmother's offer. I purchased an opulent estate in Omi Province. My days were awash with an embarrassment of riches. In all my years of privilege I'd never enjoyed luxury so great, for now no one looked over my shoulder. All decisions were mine. Yet in such freedom lay the seeds of my own humiliation.

"Because I'd never possessed so much money at once, I'd learned nothing of restraint. I squandered my gold on one trifle after another. Soon I was spending beyond my means. I employed too many servants and concubines, ate and drank to excess, caroused until all hours and slept half the daylight away.

"My story is no different than those of many other spoiled sons. A bounty is poorly guarded by one who lacks gratitude. You'll not be surprised to hear that the day quickly came when I found my coffers exhausted. Having believed wealth my unending due, I awoke from a stupor of luxury to find my fortune reduced to a heap of unpayable debts. I was soon selling off my belongings in a frantic effort to settle accounts. It was not enough. I was compelled to surrender my estate, and at length I found myself destitute.

"From the ruins I had made of my many blessings, I staggered out into the dusty streets. Before long, I came to know hunger for the first time in my life. And now I understood that I would perish if I did not find employment. But few were as unskilled as I.

"From village to village I roamed in desperation,

knocking on doors and pleading with one man after another, 'Teach me a skill and I will work faithfully!' I was turned down again and again. With no other choice, I soon began to lie, claiming myself a carpenter, a field hand, whatever it took to get a bit of work, only to bungle every job and be cast out by my justly angered employers.

"My sole worldly possession during this miserable time was Father's old scroll, which I had taken pains to keep while settling my debts. I could not bear to part with it, for it was all that remained of Father and the life he'd given me. Everywhere I went I carried the scroll wrapped in a mean oilcloth.

"One wretched rainy night, while shivering upon the dank dirt where I had made my bed beneath a bridge, I took out the scroll and read its words again by the dim moonlight:

*When you drink from a stream,
remember the spring*

"This message, which had never made sense to me, now stirred bitterness in my heart. Of what stream do I drink? I said to myself. None! My wellspring is dry. I choke in the mud of poverty! I was in such a shameful state that I muttered a curse upon my late father for bequeathing me this paper inscribed with its useless riddle. I determined then that I would sell the scroll. Perhaps it would fetch a little something.

"The next morning I stood before an antiques dealer in Sakai. As the man pored over the scroll's striking calligraphy, I noticed a quiet amazement in his eyes. He then looked me up and down in my ragged clothes, and I caught a quick change of expression as he tried to appear nonchalant. 'I'll give you three *ryo*,' he said with feigned indifference.

"Understanding the scroll's worth somewhat better now, I took it to a dealer in Osaka. In this second man's face I beheld a similar flicker of greed as he examined the scroll. But this man offered me even less than the first. When I told him I could get more from the other shop, he thought I was bluffing. Shrugging, he said, 'Sell it to me and eat well tonight, or stay hungry. It's up to you.'

"As I left the shop, the man called after me with new eagerness, doubling his offer. This I refused, only to hear him triple his sum. I kept walking. The man hurried to his doorway and called out a figure five times his original price. But now it was clear to me that the value of the scroll far exceeded anything I would be offered in my beggarly state. The scroll was indeed more precious than I could have known. And recalling how I had cursed my father's memory the night before, I suffered pangs of remorse. I uttered a prayer of gratitude to Father's wise and generous spirit.

"But to what wretchedness had I sunken since his death? First taking my stepmother's sordid bribe with no regard for the honor of Father's household, then squandering everything, and now ignoring the grave counsel Father had given me so early in life and seeking to sell the very object he'd said I should never trade. Still, the scroll seemed my last hope.

"I sat down beside the road and unrolled the ancient *washi* paper once more. I studied the calligrapher's lively strokes, as dramatic as forks of lightning. Presently I heard a voice above me.

"'There's an object worth caring for!'

"Looking up, I saw the shape of a man, silhouetted against the blinding light of the sun. I could not see his face at first, but the fine robes and sandals he wore seemed familiar, and the thought briefly seized me that he was my father come back from the afterlife.

"'A genuine Ikkyu!' said the man. 'I've beheld only one other like it in my lifetime.'

"Now he squatted before me and I saw a smooth brown face of great kindliness. The man was not my father, of course, but something in his manner still reminded me of Papa. And his robes were indeed much the same. No doubt he was a man of equal wealth and success. Sensing opportunity, I quickly gathered my thoughts.

"'Sir,' I said, 'since you obviously perceive the preciousness of this antique, perhaps you might consider buying it.'

"At this the man gave a gentle, knowing smile.

"'Oh, but you should never sell this scroll,' he said quietly. 'Its value is beyond reckoning. And not just because the calligrapher, Ikkyu, was a genius and legend among Zen masters—but because this scroll's value will grow the longer you keep it and better understand its wisdom.'

"My heart leapt upon hearing these words, for I recognized them to be almost exactly what Father had said to me so long ago. I was dumbstruck.

"The man's clean, manicured hand came forth and touched my arm. 'If you cannot be convinced to keep the scroll, I know an antiques collector who will pay you well for it. But listen, even better, would you be willing to assist me with a task today?'

"As I had guessed, he was a local merchant. He said he needed an extra hand to help his employees load a huge quantity of goods onto a buyer's train of carts.

"'I'll gladly pay you, and see that you're well fed for the day.'

"Hungry as I was, I readily agreed.

"We walked together to his estate. He told me his name was Takeo. When we'd reached his house, Takeo sat me down to a bountiful meal amongst the other employees in his kitchen. Though simple, the food looked ravishing. Overcome with gratitude, I nearly wept as I ate.

"I spent the rest of the afternoon hard at work, my arms loaded with heavy stoneware as I trudged from the stockroom to the customer's carts—back and forth for hours. But my spirits remained high. With my belly full and the promise of pay ahead, I hardly noticed my aching muscles. In fact, I was so happy I felt I could work for a month without pause.

"At day's end, Takeo drew me aside to give me my earnings. He looked into my eyes.

"'You're a hard worker, Manzo!'

"'The hardest worker you'll find in Osaka,' I said.

"'I like the energy you've shown today.'

"With a smile, he pressed several coins into my outstretched hand. I beheld a golden *ryo* glimmering among the coppers. The sight of it took my breath away. Though few had less knowledge than I of a day's rightful earnings, I knew this was far more than I deserved.

"Offering sincere thanks, I handed back the golden *ryo*, pocketed the coppers, and, at a loss for further words, made a weak gesture of farewell and turned to go. Takeo's generosity moved me profoundly, but the sight of that precious coin had roused a new determination within me: I must learn the true value of work, and stand on my own two feet in the world.

"Before I got far, Takeo called after me.

"'You know, Manzo, I've just lost an employee and could use a new worker.'

"I turned. 'Sir?'

"'Tell me,' he placed his hands on his hips and gave

me a testing look, 'what are your skills?'

"I remembered my recent experiences with the employers I'd deceived, and knew I must be honest this time. I told him, 'I fear I have no particular skills, sir, but surely no one's more eager to learn than I.'

"'You're willing to learn, are you?'

"'Indeed I am, sir!'

"The merchant smiled. 'Then don't worry. I'll see that you're well trained.'

"I could hardly believe my luck. After all my troubles, this stranger was offering me respectable employment! Hot tears flooded my eyes.

"'Well?' said Takeo, chuckling. 'Do you wish to be hired?'

"I swallowed a sob and said, 'I wish to prove more faithful than any employee you've ever known!'

"Takeo showed me to a small room and saw that I was given fresh clothing and sandals. He told me to rest for the night and be ready to work again in the morning.

"Before he left me I said to my new employer, 'Forgive me, Master Takeo, but why would you take such pains over a wretch like me? Sure, I can carry stoneware for hours, but why risk employing one who admits to lacking skills?'

"Again the merchant smiled his benevolent smile. 'Let's just say I believe wholeheartedly in the wisdom on that scroll of yours.'

"I took this opportunity to confess that the scroll's message baffled me.

"Takeo responded by gesturing for me to follow him across a courtyard into his living quarters. He brought me into a small room and waved his hand across a shrine lit with candles. On the wall above the shrine hung a scroll exactly like my father's heirloom. In its stunning calligraphy I read the selfsame words:

> *When you drink from a stream,*
> *remember the spring*

"The brushstrokes seemed to come alive before my eyes, dancing in the candlelight.

"'Manzo,' said Takeo, 'as a young man I once found myself in straits similar to yours. It was upon my first employer's wall that this scroll was hung. My master grasped its meaning full well, and his actions bore out his understanding. He took a chance on me, you see. My gratitude to him made me his hardest worker. And before he died, he entrusted me with the scroll. Soon, Manzo, you'll begin to understand the message of old Master Ikkyu—tomorrow, no doubt. For this reason I knew I couldn't go wrong in hiring you.'

"Takeo's words proved prophetic. The following morning I woke before daylight, sought out my fellow employees, and set to work amongst them in a spirit of great joy. My labors were clumsy at first, and some of the workers begrudged me this, but my enthusiasm did not diminish in the least, for I sensed that I was working for a man of noble spirit from whom I would not fail to learn much. At noontime, pausing from my labors to eat a nourishing meal, I reflected on my great fortune at finding myself employed, sheltered, and generously fed. It suddenly occurred to me that I was indeed, as Takeo had foreseen, coming to understand the truth of the scroll's words. Feelings of gratitude seemed to be making a new man of me, transforming my fate. Surely that's what came to one who 'remembered the spring,' the source of one's blessings!

"Each morning thereafter I rose a bit earlier, becoming a better worker by the day, and within a few months I had earned the distinction of the household's earliest riser. At the end of each day I found it difficult to leave off my tasks, so I began to work regularly until midnight as well. Unlike some of the other servants, I took pride in performing my duties with equal excellence whether under supervision or not.

"One day Takeo summoned me to his quarters. 'Manzo,' he said, 'I'm pleased to see that you always work faithfully, but I'd be more pleased if you would stop your work at an earlier hour and go to bed at the same time as your fellow servants. If you continue to be so much more industrious than they, there will be complaints among them.'

"'My good master,' I replied. 'I don't like to disobey you, but in truth I can never get to sleep before midnight.'

"'You're a rare one, Manzo, and I'm grateful for your zeal! But maybe you could stay in bed, at least, until the other servants get up in the morning.'

"'My good master,' I said again, 'I'm afraid I'm hopeless. I can't for the life of me stay in bed past five o'clock in the morning.'

"Now Takeo paced the floor of his quarters, thinking. At length an idea struck him. 'Manzo, you are your own master while your fellow servants are asleep. We both know that's the natural law of things. And I truly do not wish you to work for me in those hours. But since you prefer not to rest, you ought to employ that time in making sandals for your own profit. I'll see that you're provided with plenty of straw.'

"'Master Takeo, you're very kind, but I'm afraid I can't work for my own profit employing time that I might use for your benefit.'

"At this Takeo wagged a finger. 'Ah Manzo, you can't refuse all my proposals. Please do as I request just this once.'

"Naturally, I could not refuse my master's kindness, and I consented to use my spare time for my own profit. After that, my early morning and late evening hours were devoted to the task of making *waraji* straw sandals, which Takeo sold to a housewares dealer in Osaka.

"Thus I began to earn a small but regular second income, every bit of which I entrusted to my master for safekeeping. After a while the people of Izumi Province began asking for 'Manzo sandals' in preference to other types. This naturally pleased the housewares dealer and he pressed me for further supplies. Master Takeo, likewise pleased at the success of his plan, determined to lend out the money I'd entrusted to him, hoping to increase the amount by good interest. He had little difficulty in this endeavor, for people had come to believe that luck attached itself to anything connected with Takeo's sandal-making servant, and were only too glad to be accommodated with loans out of his savings.

"Ten years passed and I remained happily employed by Takeo. One day the master called me into his study again.

"'My dear Manzo,' he said. 'I can hardly believe ten years have gone by since I found you in the street studying that beautiful Ikkyu scroll.'

"'Yes, Master Takeo. How fortunate I became that day!'

"'Not you alone, Manzo. I've watched you closely over the decade you've spent in my employ. You've never squandered your wages as other servants do; after setting apart a small amount for personal expenses you've committed to my care all that you earned. I would have served poorly as your banker if I hadn't sought some profitable investment for your deposits. All these years I've been lending out your money at a moderate rate, and it's astonishing to find how much your capital now amounts to. Behold! Your savings, with interest, have reached the sum of one hundred golden *ryo!* Now, what do you propose to do with all this money?'

"I was taken aback at the idea of such wealth. 'My good master,' I said, 'you must be joking!'

"'Not at all. One hundred *ryo* it is! Will you continue to lend it out, or would you prefer to dispose of it in some other way? It's for you to decide.'

"'One hundred *ryo!*' I gasped. 'Did you really say *one hundred* ryo?'

"'One hundred *ryo!*' replied my employer, smiling.

"'It's unbelievable!'

"'Your own industry is responsible for it,' said Takeo. 'Now tell me your plans for the money.'

"I thought long and hard, and could truly summon no answer. There was nothing I felt I lacked.

"Takeo, with a look of keen approval, came close and gripped my shoulders, staring into my eyes. 'Manzo, you have a pure and grateful heart. Remember when I told you how my first employer entrusted me with the Ikkyu scroll before he died?'

"'Of course, Master Takeo.'

"'What he also entrusted to me, Manzo, was his business.'

"'Sir?'

"'The very business about which you've learned so much in your ten years under my employ. And now,

Manzo, as I am getting old and am ready for my rest, and as I have no sons, I wish to bequeath the enterprise to you.'

"'To me, sir?'

"'Indeed. It's only fitting, you see? For you've learned the truth of the scroll. Your understanding of this truth is born out by your actions every day. Your spirit is one of willing service. Now, in addition to entrusting you the business, I propose that we set you up as one of the branch families in the village. Your hundred *ryo* will easily supply you a house befitting your station. And isn't it time, Manzo, that you took a wife?'

"I felt myself blush hotly at this remark, which caused my master to laugh heartily and slap my shoulder. Takeo's business proposal astonished me. I was by no means eager to accept such a great honor. But it was clearly my employer's heartfelt wish, and I understood that I would be doing a rightful honor to his prior employer as well, so I consented.

"Soon afterward I found a wife. We had three children together. For many years my family has lived happily and our business has thrived in Osaka. Master Takeo, when he passed away some years ago, entrusted his Ikkyu scroll to my keeping. It now hangs with my father's heirloom above my family shrine. I will never part with these scrolls. I've sought to instill their wisdom in my children."

With this, Manzo concluded his account. A reverent silence gripped the many students before him.

From the edge of the assembly, a Portuguese priest called Xavier rose to his feet, resplendent in his dark-brown robe and cape. Suspended from a golden chain at his breast was a cross of polished wood. He spoke in a deep, resonant voice.

"Your tale has moved me, Sir Manzo. Gratitude lies at the heart of all the world's great spiritual traditions—my own no less than any other. I never considered that gratitude attracts luck, but how could it be otherwise? For indeed, gratitude instills a spirit of sincere and industrious service. It's been our privilege to hear your story today, Sir Manzo, and to be reminded of one of the world's great truths."

At this, Hideyoshi came forward and thanked the mustached merchant, then proposed that the temple school reconvene a fortnight hence. So the afternoon session drew to a close, and the crowd of students dispersed. But upon the sun-dappled grass beneath the trees a small crowd lingered, watching the gentle-spirited Manzo amble away shoulder-to-shoulder with Hideyoshi.

Already the merchant's teachings rested deep in the hearts of these listeners, and when at last they turned to journey home, each man among them pondered the things that made him grateful.

Know Your Gift: The Potter's Counsel

"Taro! Taro, wake up!"

Sixteen-year-old Taro stirred awake to his uncle's gruff voice and a strong hand shaking his shoulder. The boy squinted at the morning light streaming through the door beyond the old man.

"Taro, come and help me get the glaze down!"

The boy wiped his eyes and sat up. "Time for glazing already?" he said. "Why didn't you wake me sooner, Uncle Kokichi?"

The potter's grizzled face broke into a fond smile at his young nephew's eagerness, which never seemed to fade. Kokichi waved a hand. "Bah! You worked hard yesterday, so you deserve extra sleep. But come now."

To Taro it seemed Uncle spoke with uncharacteristic gentleness this morning. Usually he barked out orders with a crossness that belied his kind heart—not that Taro ever minded, for he loved and respected the old potter.

The boy stepped into his sandals and shuffled with Kokichi through the narrow little house to the pottery shop at the back. Taro gazed admiringly around. In the slatted window light stood his uncle's potting wheel, its crank handle caked with years of dried clay. At the rear of the room, the kiln fire was already burning, the familiar scent of its smoke drifting through the air. Along every wall ran shelves lined with finished pots, jars, bowls, and cups of all designs, gleaming in their rich and colorful glazes. The boy never failed to notice and appreciate Kokichi's work, each object beautiful in its mastery.

To Taro, it seemed the potter carried an old sadness deep in his soul, and labored endlessly to transform this burden into works of art. Years before, the boy knew, Kokichi had lost his wife in childbirth, and his infant son shortly thereafter. He had devoted himself to his wheel and kiln ever since. Taro admired his uncle's dedication, and was grateful to serve such an accomplished artisan.

In accordance with their silent routine, old Kokichi now mounted a creaking bamboo ladder and climbed toward the shelf where the reserves of glaze were stored. He stretched out his arms, took hold of a clay jar and lifted. Grunting, he twisted his body awkwardly on the ladder to pass the jar down to Taro. The boy received the container and turned to set it by, while Kokichi reached for another.

There was a sudden splintering noise, then a dreadful crash rang out. Taro whipped around. He gasped to see his uncle sprawled upon the floor at the foot of the ladder amid a mess of glaze and shattered clay. Blood oozed from his bald head.

For a moment Taro stood stunned. The potter's bleeding brow triggered a whirl of terrifying memories, sweeping the boy ten years into the past—to the night of the terrible earthquake that had demolished half of his family home and killed his father where he slept. Taro's mother, thrown from her feet, had struck her head on the stone hearth and been knocked unconscious. She was a weaver of mats and had intended to work late, so she'd just lighted a small whale oil lamp. Aghast, six year-old Taro watched as his mother's burning lamp clattered from the table and rolled to her store of straw. Flames leapt within seconds, and it seemed no more than a moment before the house was ablaze. The small boy was helpless to save his parents. He ran to a neighbor for help, but the fire raged too quickly and both mother and father were lost to him that night.

An orphaned peasant child, Taro had made his way from village to village toward the town of Tomikura, where his irascible uncle Kokichi took him in.

Now the boy broke free of his reverie and rushed to help the potter, who was already trying to sit up.

"Uncle, you're bleeding!"

"Am I?" To the boy's surprise, Kokichi chuckled. "I suppose I'll never become a bird and fly away with these bony wings!" The uncle flapped his elbows and laughed again. He knew well the ill fortune his young nephew had suffered, and despite his throbbing head, kept smiling to ease his charge's obvious fright. "Help me up, boy."

Taro helped the old man to his feet and drew up a stool for him. He then ran to fetch water. Returning with a cupful and a cloth, he set about cleaning the blood from Kokichi's wrinkled head.

"Goodness, Uncle, what a scare that gave me!"

Kokichi seized the boy's hand. "Taro, you're shaking."

"Yes! I thought for a moment you'd died. I don't know what I'd do, Uncle, were … such a thing to happen!"

The old potter held the boy with a deep stare. "But it *will* happen, you know. I'm not getting younger."

"Let's not talk about it, Uncle."

Old Kokichi's face took on a solemn thoughtfulness. "Boy," he said in his coarse manner, "we'd be fools not to think about it. What'll you do when I'm gone?"

Taro offered no answer. He dipped the cloth in the water once more, his face a mask of blank alarm.

"Answer me, boy!"

Timidly Taro replied, "I suppose I'll become a servant somewhere."

"Bah! What sort of man fails to pursue a trade?"

"I'm not a man, Uncle."

Kokichi gave a grumbling laugh. "You're sixteen this year, you featherhead! It's time you grew up. Tell me, what are your talents?"

"I've no particular talents. I'm grateful to serve."

"No talents? More nonsense still! Someday you'll want a family of your own, won't you? Then you must know your gift, boy, and work to develop it!" Kokichi waved the boy's hand away. "Stop that now. It's not bleeding anymore."

The boy drew back and the potter leaned forward on his stool. His eyes had a watery softness Taro had never seen before.

"Listen. You help me greatly by running errands and buying supplies, tending the shop and delivering orders. I've watched you all the time you've lived with me, and now you mean to say you have no gift?"

"It seems so, Uncle."

"But of course you have, boy!"

"I do?"

"Yes!"

"What is it, Uncle?"

The potter grumbled again. "I have to tell you, do I? Very well. Your gift, Taro, is your unfailing persistence."

"Persistence?"

"Yes, boy! You stick to your labors, no matter how wearying. That's a gift!"

Taro looked confused. "I've never thought of such a thing as a gift, Uncle. But maybe it is. Tell me then, how will I find my trade?"

Kokichi turned a palm upward. "Best try your hand at pottery."

"But surely I lack the skill to become a master

potter like you."

The old man furrowed his wounded brow. "Listen to me, boy! If you've the brains to understand, hark with deep attention." Taking hold of his nephew's shoulders, the old potter uttered words that would alter the young man's destiny: "Five years makes a living, ten years makes a master."

Kokichi fixed a probing gaze upon the boy, who still appeared puzzled.

"Five years from now you'll be twenty-one," said the uncle. He turned and swept a hand toward his shelves of finished pottery, each cup and bowl exquisite in its own right. "Will you be a servant, Taro, or a potter?"

Kokichi did not belabor the point, but his simple message was worth a lifetime of speeches, for it carried the power to pierce Taro's mind, and the young man felt his eyes opening to a new vision of the future. He bowed his head and shed grateful tears as he humbly agreed to become Kokichi's apprentice.

That day marked the boy's initiation into manhood, the start of a long journey toward self-respect. As Taro had predicted, he was clumsy and slow in learning the trade. He bungled the glazing and firing, and wasted much clay. Many were the times Kokichi shouted and swore at him. But just as the potter foresaw, over time his nephew grew competent—and confident.

And soon the boy noticed a strange and pleasant sensation accompanying his working days. Before now, he'd always believed himself devoid of natural gifts, and held no desire to learn the art of ceramics. It had seemed enough to simply admire his uncle's talents. But gradually Taro discovered that careful attention to one's work begets love for it. He came to understand more deeply his particular gift of devoting himself completely to a task.

Five years passed away, the fields around Tomikura shifting hues from emerald to bronze to emerald again, and with his twenty-first year Taro had become fully proficient in the potter's craft, just as Kokichi had foreseen. He and the old man took on a servant and a new apprentice.

Another five years came and went. Five times over, Tomikura's great chestnut trees shed their canopies and blossomed anew, as they had for over eighty seasons. In Taro's tenth spring as a potter Kokichi proclaimed his young partner a master. That same year a wealthy Spanish importer came to favor the large rice bowls fired in the shop, and decided to contract a standing order. The old potter drew his nephew aside.

"It's your special glazing style that's caught the Spaniard's eye. You must take advantage of this fellow's interest, Taro, and start your own enterprise."

"My own? What do you mean, Uncle?"

Kokichi smiled wistfully. "This old shop is too small for you now. Besides, I'll be retiring by the end of the year. Your time has arrived, Taro."

So the nephew heeded his uncle's advice, contracted with the Spaniard, and had soon established his own pottery shop, as well as a separate manufacturing and exporting facility. Within a few years he employed twenty-four workers. By then Taro had taken a wife and was blessed with a son and daughter. His wife cared for the aging Kokichi like her own father, and the old man was as a grandfather to their children.

By and by came the hour that old Kokichi passed from this life. Taro was kneeling at his uncle's bedside. Moments before the potter departed, he squeezed his one-time assistant's hand with his gnarled fingers and said, "Nephew, you've become my son in these years we've spent laboring side by side. And how proud it's made me to watch you become a master!"

"Father Kokichi," said Taro—for he had long since regarded the old potter as his parent—"without you I would never have understood how men differ in the nature of their gifts, and in their abilities to perceive them. From you I've learned the wisdom of taking counsel from a knowledgeable man when one is unsure of one's talents. From you I've learned the value in thinking not of *having* a gift, but of *developing* one. And now I understand that all men of grateful spirit can achieve success if they work to make the most of their talents. Indeed, any man who will devote five years of hard work and study to a trade will become proficient enough to earn his living thereby, and any man who devotes ten years of hard work and study to a trade will become a master. By your wisdom, Father Kokichi, you've enriched my life beyond description."

So saying, the young master potter fell silent. His old father and teacher, with a blissful smile, had drifted away into the next world.

発想 7

Conceivable Means Achievable: Nobunaga the "Fool"

*I*n the twilight, the elm trees outside Soganji Temple began to sway with a soft breeze, hinting of the cooler night to come. A crowd of eager students, having gathered after their long day's labor, settled upon the grass. Since the prior session their numbers had swelled, for numerous passersby had found themselves irresistibly drawn to the gathering, and had tarried to listen.

Amidst the studentship there was much chatter. It was said Hideyoshi had invited a distinguished visitor to speak, and rumors were afloat that Hideyoshi's superior, Lord Nobunaga, was to be the subject of this evening's discussion. Or had Hideyoshi invited the lord himself? Either way, surely some secret insight into Nobunaga's brilliance would be gleaned by all who listened tonight. And what man could fail to benefit from such knowledge? Nobunaga's feats were legendary, and had made him Japan's *shogun*—in deed if not yet in name. His fiercely loyal retainers regarded him as a god of war.

Now Hideyoshi came forward and introduced

Hanshiro, a dignified samurai of sixty-one years who walked slowly but steadily to the speaking stump. Hanshiro bowed, arranged his brown and black robes beneath him, then sat and surveyed the assembly. His head was shaved in the *sakayaki* style, with a topknot in back, and his high, hairless brow glistened in the bluish evening light.

"Forty-one summers have passed," he began, "since my first season as a servant to Lord Nobunaga. In the decades between then and my retirement some years ago, I came to know the lord as you all do now: a man whose name is destined to endure forever."

Hanshiro observed many students nodding in solemn agreement.

"But there was once a time when people scoffed at our master. Indeed, they even dubbed him 'Lord Fool.' Despite his early skills as a fighter, and his passionate boyhood interest in all things martial, few could have predicted he would rise above his father's station as assistant deputy of Owari Province."

A murmur of surprise rose from the crowd. Who could believe Nobunaga had ever been anything less than a formidable and ingenious warrior?

"Listen," continued the distinguished old lecturer, "and I will explain how a boy, once called 'fool' by many, rose to become the ruler we fear and admire. As Sir Hideyoshi says so astutely, *Conceivable Means Achievable*, and Nobunaga's towering achievements owe much to his grasp of this secret."

With a grunt, Hanshiro drew his legs up beneath him, Buddha-like. He planted a hand at each knee and sat back on his haunches with the sage and dignified air of a man who knew much of the world. No doubt he'd sat at many a war counsel in exactly the same posture.

As he spoke, old Hanshiro's voice ranged artfully through pitches low and high, from guttural rasps to eloquent warbles, which held his listeners entranced.

"One day in Nobunaga's thirteenth year," Hanshiro recounted, "he was strutting through Nagoya's town market in the company of a few friends. The adolescent Nobunaga had developed some strange habits. Everywhere he went he carried a long bamboo spear rather than the sword of a proper samurai. And recently he and his cronies had taken up the outlandish pastime of darting between the cluttered market stalls, impaling melons as if the spheres of fruit were their enemies. While the boys staged attacks upon this or that pile of goods, the mortified vendors could only stand by and watch. Then Nobunaga, laughing, would fling a coin or two in payment for the damage. It was this flamboyant misconduct that had caused many townspeople to begin whispering unflatteringly about the young 'Lord Fool.'

"On this particular day, Nobunaga had just tossed a silver coin to a merchant when his ears pricked up at the sound of a nearby vendor hawking goods: 'Persimmons! Fresh persimmons from Mino Province here!'

"'Mino Province!' Nobunaga said to himself. 'Why, that's the realm of my father's rival.'

"The young 'fool' approached the merchant and purchased three persimmons.

"'And here's a bit extra,' he said quietly, slipping the vendor a coin, 'if you tell me of goings-on in Mino.'

"The merchant accepted the coin, looked suspiciously about, then bade Nobunaga follow him to the rear of his stall. There the merchant spoke of Dosan, the so-called Viper of Mino.

"'The fruit suppliers say Dosan started as an oil peddler. He rose to power through pure talent, cunning, and ruthlessness. Now he's infamous in Mino for his cruelty. They say he boils his foes in vats of oil.'

"'I want to know his plans,' said Nobunaga. 'Sell me more Mino persimmons,' he winked, 'and you'll be well paid.'

"In this way, Nobunaga began learning about his father's enemy. By conceiving this simple plan to gather intelligence, our lord took the first step toward his eventual triumphs.

"Till then, Nobunaga's powerful talents had remained unfocused and had only served to vex those around him, leading the young man into trouble time and again.

"I can tell you that even in infancy, Nobunaga's spirit had been unconquerable. I remember the tremendous squalls coming from his nursery day and night, not to mention the shrieks of the poor nursemaids, whose nipples he would bite with bestial ferocity. Oh, the household hired nurse after nurse until every full-bosomed matron within a mile of Nagoya Castle had felt the sting of 'milk duty'!"

Hanshiro slapped his thigh at the thought of his lord's boundless energy, exhibited so early in life. The old samurai's stately chuckles spread through the crowd of listeners.

"Well, by the time Nagoya Castle's wild infant grew to be a rambunctious ten-year-old, his father had recognized the child's extraordinary vitality as a hallmark to be cherished. Rightfully so, for Nobunaga exhibited more than mere rowdiness. His gifts in the martial arts were clear to everyone from his earliest days of idle swordplay. Indeed, the father glimpsed a future leader in this boy, but knew that a spirit so lively would require conscientious training. So the father charged his most faithful vassal, Masahide, with the task of educating Nobunaga.

"Masahide met the challenge with zest, and did all in his power to instruct the child and harness his talents, but with each passing year Nobunaga seemed only to grow more contrary. Masahide was often at a loss to reprimand him. The boy's fierce intelligence and relentless stubbornness proved obstacles greater than any teacher could surmount.

"So throughout Nobunaga's youth, the problem had remained this: the young man felt driven by an inherent greatness of spirit, but had never precisely defined this greatness, nor conceived of how it could benefit his family or his province. Everything changed, at last, on this day at the market in Nobunaga's thirteenth year, for it was then that he formulated his first conceivable goal. His foolish behavior could serve as a tactic for gathering information on his father's behalf. No one suspected a fool!

"The boy's father had reason to be uneasy in those dark days. Dissension roiled his clan, and many families considered his favorite son an unfit heir. One faction already schemed to position another young man in Nobunaga's place. And always Owari Province was threatened by the notorious Viper of Mino.

"But now, aided by the intelligence Nobunaga gathered in the markets and public squares, his father prepared to wage a campaign against the Viper. And so it came to pass that a year later, Nobunaga, at the age of fourteen, distinguished himself in his first battle, fighting fearlessly under his sire's sword.

"Ultimately, however, the tide of war turned against them. Our young lord saw a great many men struck down around him. Defeated, Nobunaga's father was forced to reconcile with his hated foe. To protect his fiefdom from retaliation he arranged, after long negotiations, a diplomatic marriage between his own family and that of his enemy. Nobunaga would be betrothed to Princess Noh, the Viper's daughter.

"As Masahide broached the news to his ungovernable charge, Nobunaga cut him short with a laugh. 'Ha! Me marry? Think again, teacher!'

"'But don't you wish to know,' said Masahide patiently, 'who your bride would be?'

"'I'll choose my own bride!' answered the young man, his eyes flashing fiercely.

"'It is Princess Noh,' said the teacher, and stood by, watching his pupil with a buried smile. Masahide knew Nobunaga could not deny the strategic benefits of the betrothal. Sure enough, the rebellious young lord now assumed an air of calm dignity.

"'Very well, it's best for all,' said Nobunaga softly. In that moment he'd recognized that the marriage would be an important step toward a worthy end: the unification of two provinces.

"Our master was fifteen years old and Princess Noh fourteen the day they married. It was a good union, and Nobunaga soon appeared to settle down and devote himself seriously to martial pursuits.

"One day on the streets of Nagoya he encountered a gun merchant and requested a firearms demonstration on the castle grounds. The power of the new weapons impressed the young lord deeply.

"Standing amid drifting plumes of black gun smoke, his ears ringing from the deafening reports, he said to himself, This is how we'll unify Owari Province and conquer fiefdoms beyond. Though Father does not command great legions of men, this weaponry will empower us beyond our numbers!

"Nobunaga had arrived at another important conception—and one that would prove achievable for a young man so prodigiously gifted. But the realization of this vision would be delayed, for presently tragedy struck.

"A terrible illness seized Nobunaga's father, and the good deputy died at the age of forty-two. Profound grief overtook his son. Given his proud nature, the young lord found such inner pain impossible to express. He shut himself away.

"At the funeral, the heads of many families awaited the late master's favored heir. Tradition held that the first son to offer incense at the altar would succeed the family. When the time arrived, Nobunaga had yet to appear. Banshoji Temple began to echo with whispers.

"A scowling family elder lumbered up to Nobunaga's guardian. 'Masahide, where in heaven's name is young Master Nobunaga?'

"The teacher, as ever, was at a loss to account for his charge.

"'The time is well past,' said the elder. Turning, he nodded to Nobuyuki, the young man the disgruntled families favored as successor. Nobuyuki jumped up and started toward the altar.

"Just then a commotion was heard at the back

of the temple. With reckless haste, Nobunaga came charging through the company of guests. A wave of indignation arose at the sight of him, for he wore a plain robe and not the formal *hakama* trousers required for the solemn occasion. What's more, a longsword was thrust through his belt!"

Here the old samurai Hanshiro paused from his tale, smiling wryly atop the speaking stump as a buzz of dismay passed through Hideyoshi's temple school.

"Well, it's no wonder you're shocked to hear of our master's behavior on that day," Hanshiro chuckled. "Though surely his actions were inexcusable, they were yet another mark of the irrepressible personality which would distinguish him as a leader. And hear this: the young eccentric strode straight past Nobuyuki to stand before his father's altar. The rival drew back.

"For a moment Nobunaga remained motionless, head bowed, and a tense silence gripped the temple. The young lord's face, illumined by the flickering candles, was contorted in grief. Then he reached into the bronze censer and brought forth a handful of incense powder. All waited for the ceremonial gesture, but instead of sprinkling an offering into the flames, Nobunaga swept his arm violently across the altar and the spraying incense snuffed both candles. Amid the gasps of the funeral guests he turned and bounded from the temple.

"Every last mourner stood rigid with shock. All

traces of solemnity, of decorum, of tradition had been shattered. Then the heads of the rival families began to shout.

"'An outrage!'

"'Idiot!'

"'Nobunaga is no successor!'

"The family elder again approached Masahide, fuming. 'Sir Masahide,' he thundered, so all could hear, 'as guardian, you must take responsibility for Nobunaga's disgraceful behavior!' Then he and his allies stalked out of Banshoji Temple.

"Masahide, leaving the temple after them, could only shake his head in despair.

"Well, Nobunaga took his official place as successor, but it seemed the heart had gone out of him. Dissenting factions of the family continued to support Nobuyuki as the rightful heir. Discord threatened to tear the clan apart.

"Nobunaga spent his days brooding in his castle quarters. Distracted by his own emotions, he appeared to lack a clear purpose and had yet to seize leadership as he should. Was he paralyzed by grief at the death of his father? Repeatedly Masahide urged the young lord to conform himself to the demands of his station and assume the proper air of authority, but this counsel went unheeded.

"By and by came a gray afternoon when Nobunaga was practicing with spears in the castle courtyard, and a courier hurried toward him across the grounds. Breathlessly the messenger delivered a grievous dispatch.

"'Masahide has slit his belly in ritual *seppuku* before his family grave!'"

Now old Hanshiro's listeners sent up a collective gasp. The last of the twilight had turned to darkness and a few torches had been lit near the speaking stump. In the flickering orange light, the samurai's shadow loomed across the mesmerized students.

"No one knows for certain," Hanshiro continued, "but it seems Masahide sacrificed himself in a final plea to Nobunaga. And indeed, this tragedy awakened resolve in the young lord. I remember the solemn determination that possessed him after that day. Everyone could see the new sharpness in his hawkish gaze. None of us knew at the time, but the shock of his teacher's demise had brought him to conceive, at last, of his ultimate goal."

Hanshiro's voice quavered solemnly as he recalled the historic moment, and he nodded with a proud, emphatic slowness.

"So that the message of Masahide's death would not go unheeded, Nobunaga vowed that he himself and no one else would pacify the whole of Owari Province. Whereupon he would conquer Mino Province—and after that unite all of Japan's splintered kingdoms! And he saw that the first conceivable step toward this grand aim would be to uproot the dissension in his own family.

"Nobunaga at last became a visionary that day. Since then, our lord's life has never failed to bear out the truth of Sir Hideyoshi's third secret, *Conceivable Means Achievable*, for there was no stopping Nobunaga when he harnessed his prodigious gifts to a clear objective. To honor his deceased guardian, he built Masahide Temple, which still stands in Nagoya. Then he slew his rival Nobuyuki, went on to unify Owari Province, and conquered his way to Kyoto.

"Our master's immense goal was conceivable for a simple reason. He recognized how he might use his gift of unconventional thought to great strategic effect. While other warlords drafted armies of farmers and were thus compelled to plan campaigns around the agrarian calendar, Nobunaga organized the first professional army deployable year-round. Remembering the firearms demonstration he'd witnessed before his father's death, he became the first to purchase guns in quantity, and the first to train musket brigades in volley firing—a tactic used to devastating effect at the Battle of Nagashino."

"Indeed!" came a voice from the rear of the assembly. "I can speak to that, for I, too, fought at Nagashino—against Lord Nobunaga."

All heads turned to find Daizen the *ronin* rising to his feet.

"I'll never forget the sight of your master's gunners lined up three deep behind their pickets, muskets at the ready—nor the tremendous blasts that met our charge, and how quickly our mounted samurai fell while Nobunaga's marvelous black and white banners fluttered above." Daizen's eyes gleamed with the memory. "Though I lost my own master to the power of those guns, I knew even then that our opponent was a leader of fearsome brilliance!"

"Yes, my friend," said Hanshiro. "And not only a powerful fighter, Nobunaga was an ingenious commander, the first among warlords to hire and promote based on merit, not pedigree. Small wonder able samurai from kingdoms throughout the realm now flock to enter his service, as did our teacher Sir Hideyoshi. Today, Nobunaga's simple conceptions have brought him to the brink of achieving his ultimate goal. Really, who can deny that this one-time 'fool' is Japan's true *shogun?* The secret of his triumph lies in these words: *Conceivable Means Achievable.*"

With a proud smile, Hanshiro left the speaking stump, and the temple school adjourned.

Fireflies weaved through the dark air as the students arose and scattered, some ambling toward the temple gates, others lingering on the grassy grounds to talk.

The peasants Jiro and Gonsuke, together with their new friend Daizen, set off down the road to Miwa Village. Several other students joined them. While the *mee-mee-mee* of the cicadas droned in the surrounding trees, the students debated Hanshiro's lesson amongst themselves. Not all were swayed by the samurai's words. One peasant, a mushroom farmer, scuffed the ground with his foot, dissatisfaction darkening his features.

"Tonight's story was meant to inspire, but compared to Nobunaga we're like ants before a giant. I can marvel at his excellency's grand conceptions, but I've no idea what I might achieve."

"Likewise," said a cloth weaver. "I'm no genius warlord, just an ordinary man. How am I supposed to conceive of great goals?"

"I know how you feel," said Jiro to the two skeptics, "to you and me and to our friends, what's achievable is nothing so historic as Nobunaga's feats. But maybe achievable means something different to every person."

"Yes!" cried Gonsuke. "We all must begin where beginning is conceivable. Even Lord Nobunaga did not start out with a vision to unify Japan. First he achieved what was simple and possible: gathering intelligence."

"Indeed!" added Daizen. "Nobunaga's victories came gradually and required discipline. It's no different for any of us. Success builds upon success."

But some men grow timid at the notion of changing their destinies. So the two skeptics were hard to convince, and at a fork in the road they turned away with heads hung low, murmuring doubtfully to each other. The peasants from Miwa and their friend the *ronin,* however, continued to talk amongst themselves, and their bright voices trailed off into the mild night.

Effort Determines Results: The Vengeful Priest

"Scoundrel!" boomed Lord Sasaki, turning with fury to his retainer Jun. "You've defiled my sandals!"

Emerging from his castle pavilion into the white winter air, Lord Sasaki had just slipped his feet into his *geta* wooden clogs, only to have an unnatural warmth greet his soles. Warmth? But how could the *geta* be warm when more than hour prior he had left them on the step in the freezing weather? The snow was falling fast over the castle grounds even now. As far as the hot-tempered Sasaki was concerned, there could be only one answer. The lord's face burned blood-red as he raged at small, lanky Jun, who stood shivering in the snow before him.

"Instead of standing by and bearing the cold like an honorable attendant, Jun, you have taken your ease upon my sandals! This is a gross insult!"

Dumbstruck, Jun looked about at the other retainers. Surely one of them had seen how the snowflakes fell on his lordship's *geta,* and how, noticing this, he'd picked up the sandals and devotedly stowed them in the bosom of his garment to warm them. But the retainers stood by wordlessly as Lord Sasaki berated the hapless attendant. And then, before Jun could speak, the master kicked off one of the clogs and used it to strike him a heavy blow between the eyes. "Wretch, take that!"

Jun sprawled backward onto the icy ground, his face bloodied, his vision blurred.

"You're dismissed!" roared the master.

The second *geta* wheeled through the air and knocked Jun flat on his back. He lay bleeding in the white drifts as Lord Sasaki walked proudly across the snowy castle grounds to his quarters, barefooted, for he was in too great a rage to wait until another pair of *geta* could be brought.

The crowd of retainers vanished. No one stayed to look after Jun. None cared what became of him. For some time he lay as he had fallen, but presently the cold brought him back to consciousness, and he rose with difficulty to his feet, having bruised himself in his fall.

He picked up the first *geta* that had struck him. As tears mingled with the blood on his face, he gazed mournfully at the clog. Then the thought of his master's injustice overcame him and he gnashed his teeth in impotent rage.

"Haughty brute that you are, Sasaki," he muttered, "you shall see that you've wronged a vassal whose only wish has been to serve you honorably. I've been one of your most devoted attendants, and now because of your arrogance and reckless judgment I'm not only publicly shamed, but robbed of the position I've worked so faithfully to earn. The bond between us as lord and servant is now broken forever! I will never rest, Sasaki, till I have won back the respect I deserve, and have shown you what sore injustice you've wrought here today!"

Again Jun put the *geta* into his bosom, though now with entirely different intention, and made his way out of the castle grounds, limping painfully through the village.

From that time forth Jun's mind blazed with the single thought of revenge. He would acquire worldly distinction and find occasion to bring the brutish noble to public shame. 'Lord Sasaki must be a fool,' people would say, 'to have terminated such a brilliant and irreplaceable figure as Jun!'

Jun thought hard. How to go about attaining his goal? How, especially now that he'd been reduced to masterless poverty? Were he a stronger man, and skilled in the martial arts, he might set out to become a samurai, but he knew such a thing was inconceivable. He was no warrior. Suddenly inspiration struck. The priesthood! With effort, anyone high or low could become a priest, and the prospects of that profession were boundless. There was no distinction within the priesthood to which even the lowly and feeble might not aspire. Why, a priest with a reputation for wisdom might win access to the Court and gain notice of the Emperor himself!

Jun set out at once for Kamakura, where he entered Kenchoji, one of the Five Mountain Zen temples, as an acolyte.

The path of a Zen novice was not easy. Before he could be received into the priesthood he was compelled to endure all forms of asceticism, self-denial, and penance. Furthermore, he had to serve his superiors' every whim, performing the most menial tasks at their command. Jun, naturally, had a hard time of it. Slaving in the temple fields harvesting rice by day, toiling in the temple refectory by evening, he slept only two to three hours each night.

After some months of this ceaseless labor his weary body almost failed him. Struggling to endure the long fasts, and to turn his mind away from bodily pains, his spirit began to weaken. At last he came to his lowest point. It seemed his racked nerves could bear no more.

One evening during this time, seeing the state the acolyte was in, a wise elder priest called Taiki drew the young man aside and counseled him thus:

"Jun, you should not be surprised to find yourself so soon worn out. I've observed your labors closely, my son. In body you toil faithfully, but in spirit you merely act a role. You see, Jun, you're putting forth only average effort. Such effort can produce only average results. But if you wish to become a priest, you must exert extraordinary effort, which yields extraordinary results. This means devoting yourself to your labors body and soul. Ask yourself, my son, are you determined to endure every hardship in order to attain the end you've dreamt of?"

At these words Jun felt his will greatly bolstered, and that night as he slogged along on hands and knees, polishing the monastery's wooden hallway floors, he said to himself, A man of ordinary perseverance might have succumbed and given up by now, but I am no ordinary man! *Average effort produces average results, but extraordinary effort produces extraordinary results!*

Soon thereafter Jun acquired the habit, before collapsing to sleep at night, of looking in a mirror at the reflection of the scar on his brow. Then he would draw from a hiding place Lord Sasaki's bloodied *geta* and tell himself: Courage! Remember the arrogant lord whose injustice you will set aright! Your work is not yet done! With this, Jun's strength and calm would return, and he would go to sleep prepared to undertake the following day's labors.

Thanks to his renewed determination, Jun began to rise in the favor of his superiors, and his learning showed marked progress. At length, he thought he might advance faster if he went to another monastery. So he set his sights on the Temple of Enryakuji on Mt. Hiei, the largest and most renowned of all places of sacred teaching in Japan. Applying for admission, he was readily accepted.

Within three years' time at Enryakuji, Jun had entered the priesthood and had assumed the new name of Kembo. Slowly and surely, by concerted efforts, Kembo made himself known far and near for his deep learning and his strict commitment to a life of austere piety.

Years passed—ten and then twenty went by. Presently, on a day in his second decade at Enryakuji, Kembo was discouraged to realize that he was still far from being in a position to attract the emperor and thereby wreak revenge upon his old nemesis Lord Sasaki.

I've reached a plateau, he told himself, but I must climb still higher. I must attain world-fame if I'm to accomplish the goal I set myself long ago!

The words of the elder priest Taiki still rang in his heart: *Average effort produces average results, but extraordinary effort produces extraordinary results.*

I have put forth great effort, Kembo said to himself, but I must exert myself even more to achieve my aim. Indeed, I must travel to China, justly regarded as the fountainhead of all knowledge and wisdom. Yes, I will acquire all that China can impart of the Buddhist faith!

So within a few weeks Kembo sailed from his native shores. After long journeying he found himself among a strange people. Here he remained ten years. During this time Kembo visited many famous temples, studied China's sacred lore, and gathered wisdom from countless monks and teachers of profound learning. At last the fame of the Japanese priest reached the ear of the Chinese Emperor, who was pleased to grant Kembo an audience, and graciously bestowed on him a new holy name derived from one of China's leading religious figures: Mumon, or "Gateless Gate." Thus it happened that Kembo left his native country as a priest of acknowledged wisdom, but returned ten years later recognized as the foremost holy man in Japan.

After his return to Japan, Mumon stayed at the Five Mountain temple in Kamakura where he had first begun as an acolyte many years before. He'd heard nothing of Lord Sasaki for some years and was anxious to learn what had become of him. It was an unpleasant surprise to hear that the pompous Sasaki had also risen in the world. Now, as master of an enormous fiefdom, Sasaki was considered one of the most important men of the day. Not only did he hold a high office at Court, but as chief of the northeastern warlords, even the *shogun* had to treat him with respect. Mumon saw that he would have to bide his time and act warily.

He did not have long to wait. A serious illness struck the Emperor, a sickness so grave that the skill of the wisest physician proved of no use. The foremost officials of the Imperial Household met to discuss the matter. They concluded that an appeal must be made to Heaven itself on the Emperor's behalf. Who was the priest with a character so stainless, wisdom so profound, that he might be entrusted with this high mission?

One name rose to all lips.

So Mumon found himself summoned to the palace and ordered to pray to the heavenly powers for the Emperor's healing. For seven days and seven nights the priest isolated himself from all mankind in the Hall of the Blue Dragon. For seven days and seven nights he fasted and prayed. And his prayers were heard. The Emperor took a turn for the better. So rapid was his recovery that in a very short time all cause of anxiety about him was over.

His Majesty's gratitude knew no bounds. Mumon was honored with the Emperor's confidence, and soon all the ministers and courtiers were vying with each other to please and flatter the Emperor's favorite priest. Appointed head of the imperial temple, the priest received yet another name: Soshin-Daizenji.

After more than thirty years of effort, thought the priest exultantly, my goal is now within reach! It only remains to find the opportune moment for my revenge on Lord Sasaki.

But indeed, more than three decades had passed—each marking long seasons of extraordinary determination—since the lowly sandal-bearer Jun had vowed to undo the wrong of his haughty master. And the man's extraordinary study of the holy scriptures, his long vigils, his asceticism and meditation had not failed to produce an extraordinary result within him. Jun had become Kembo, then Mumon, and now

Soshin-Daizenji, and his character had undergone a correspondingly radical change, though he'd hardly suspected it. His mind had been purified and was now incapable of harboring so mean and paltry a feeling as a grudge over an old insult. Now that the power to avenge was in his grasp he realized he no longer cared to exercise it.

To hate, or to try to injure a fellow creature, he said to himself, is below one who has entered the priesthood. I have nursed a grudge against Lord Sasaki for over thirty years. With the sole object of revenge, I've raised myself to my present position. And now I see clearly: if Lord Sasaki had not ill-treated me on that day so long ago, what would my life have been? I would probably have remained Jun, the lowly retainer, all my days. But because of my resolve to punish Sasaki, I turned priest, studied diligently, endured hardships, and now I have become one of the most influential holy men in the realm, before whom even princes and nobles bow with reverence. If I look at the matter in its true light it is to Lord Sasaki that I owe everything. Therefore, it should be gratitude and brotherly love, not revenge, that I harbor in my heart for Sasaki, for it was his unjust act that first instilled determination in me. How clear it is to me now! I've made extraordinary efforts and indeed, they've produced extraordinary results—a harvest beyond imagining, for I've gained a change of heart!

Thus the good priest relinquished his long cherished idea of vengeance. He now looked upon the bloodstained *geta* with reverence, offering flowers and burning incense before it, while day and night he prayed fervently for the long life and happiness of his old master Sasaki.

And Sasaki himself?

At the age of sixty-three he retired from public life to pass the evening of his days at his castle. During this time, he set about restoring a nearby temple, which had fallen into decay. He then desired to place a priest of deep learning and acknowledged virtue in charge. At a gathering of his chief retainers, he asked, "Who is the greatest priest of the day?"

"Soshin-Daizenji, High Priest of the Imperial Temple, is undoubtedly the greatest," came the unanimous reply.

So Sasaki decided to offer the vacant post to the holy Soshin-Daizenji. The Emperor himself agreed to Lord Sasaki's request for the service of his highest priest, and it came about that Soshin-Daizenji was appointed head of Lord Sasaki's temple.

On the seventh day after the honored priest's installation, Sasaki paid a formal call to welcome the new arrival. He was ushered into the head priest's private guestroom, which was at the moment unoccupied. Turning to the alcove, Sasaki found himself staring at an old garden *geta* placed on a stand of elaborate and costly workmanship.

What celebrated figure has used that *geta?* said the astonished Sasaki to himself. Surely it's a breach of etiquette to decorate a room with such a lowly object when about to receive a lord of my standing! But the priest must have some purpose for allowing so strange an infringement of good manners.

Just then the sliding door opened noiselessly. A venerable man in full canonical robes entered. His immobile face was that of an ascetic but marred by a disfiguring scar on his forehead between the eyes.

Soshin-Daizenji seated himself opposite his guest. Putting both hands palms downwards on the mats, he bowed several times in respectful greeting. Sasaki returned the courtesy.

When the salutations were over, Sasaki could no longer restrain his curiosity. "Your Reverence," he began. "I don't know how to thank you for agreeing to serve as priest in this temple. I am a plain man and unskilled in words. But there are two things that puzzle me. May I ask you to explain the place of honor you've given to a garden *geta,* and the scar on your brow that seems more suited to a warring man than to one of saintliness like yourself?"

Soshin-Daizenji smiled at these words, for they were poured out with the rashness he remembered in Sasaki as a young man. Tears glistened in the priest's eyes. "What joy it gives me to see your face again,

Lord Sasaki. Your unchanged features remind me of my youth."

"What? Your words are strange! How can I remind you of your youth when we never met till today?"

"My lord, have patience, and I will explain all." So Soshin-Daizenji recalled himself to his old master, and in detail told all that had befallen him since the snowy day of his dismissal more than thirty years before. He did not censor his words, but told of the injustice Lord Sasaki had wrought by shaming so faithful a servant on that day. And Soshin-Daizenji described how, through all the years since then, he had been motivated by a desire to win public distinction and thereby come to a position from which he might take revenge on his former master.

"At length, however, I came to see my journey in a different light," he said, "and to look upon you as my benefactor. If it weren't for you, the stores of knowledge in my command would never have come within my reach. I would never have studied with the illustrious holy men of two great nations. I've made extraordinary efforts in these last thirty years, my lord, and they've produced extraordinary results, for now I have only a heartfelt desire for your long life and prosperity. I pray daily that I may somehow, in some small way, pay back the great fortune you bestowed on me. Your lordship now understands why I so treasure an old *geta*, and why I happily bear this ugly scar on my brow."

Sasaki had listened to the priest's story with growing wonder and deepest attention.

"Your Reverence," he said in a voice trembling with emotion, "I can just recall the incident you mention and I remember how angry I felt, in my arrogance, over what I thought was a gross insult. I do not wonder at your determination to right that injustice. But for you to renounce your long-cherished goal in the end—that, indeed, amazes me! It is surely as you say, your astonishing effort has produced an astonishing result! I humbly beg your pardon for my past offense, and request that you enroll me as one of your disciples!"

In this way, Lord Sasaki repented of the injustice he'd committed in his youth, and a hearty friendship sprang up between the two men. The lowly sandal-bearer had achieved a greater result than he had ever dreamed of in his earliest efforts. Till death parted them many years later, Lord Sasaki and the priest saw much of each other and their affection grew boundless.

協力 9

Collaboration Breeds Success: The Guns of Tanegashima 🌿

On a sweltering July evening students gathered one last time on the knoll of Soganji Temple, eager to hear Hideyoshi's fifth and final lesson in prosperity.

Presently Koroku the giant appeared, and all strained to get a glimpse of his small master as the two made their way through the crowd. Then Hideyoshi climbed atop the speaking stump and greeted the students with a cheery salutation. The assembly bowed as one, returning a hearty "Good evening!"

"My friends," said the teacher, "tonight we examine the Fifth Secret of fortune and fulfillment. Let's begin by recalling the wise words of Motonari, the great clan chieftain of Aki Province. Who among you can relate the story of the Three Arrows?"

A new student rose and bowed respectfully toward the little samurai. He introduced himself as Handa, a pilgrim-warrior on a quest to perfect his Swordless Style of fencing. He'd been passing through Nagahama when word of Hideyoshi's temple school reached his ears.

"Master Motonari had three sons," Handa began.

"He was determined that these brothers work together, for dangerous enemies flanked their clan to east and west, and rivalries within the family could not be tolerated. One day Motonari called the three boys into his garden and handed each a single arrow.

"'Break your arrow,' he ordered each boy in turn.

"The eldest snapped his arrow with ease. The second son also had no difficulty. Even the youngest managed after some effort to break the arrow given him.

"'Well done!' said the father. 'A lone arrow is readily broken.'

"Then he produced a trio of arrows tied together with string, and handed it to his youngest. 'Now break this,' he commanded.

"The small boy strained till his face was red, but could not snap the arrows. Next the second son took up the bundle, with the same result. Finally the oldest and strongest boy expended a mighty effort, but succeeded only in slightly bending the shafts."

Hanshiro bowed and took his seat again. Hideyoshi thanked the speaker, then looked out over the studentship. "Who can state the moral of this story?"

Answers rang across the knoll.

"Strength in numbers!"

"Stand alone at your peril!"

The teacher smiled knowingly. "The ancients had many ways of saying it, and here is mine: *Collaboration Breeds Success*. No man can succeed alone. Every suc-

Collaboration Breeds Success: The Guns of Tanegashima 157

cessful person must work with others in order to achieve his goals."

Now Hideyoshi nodded to a rough-looking workman sitting nearby. The workman stood and bowed deeply. He appeared to be about fifty years of age.

Hideyoshi said, "I've asked the blacksmith Goro to speak this evening. Listen carefully if you aspire to grasp the fifth and final secret!"

The man called Goro moved to the speaking stump and took his seat before the students. His broad, cleft chin sprouted a spiny patch of gray hair. With unhurried composure he smoothed his black vest, then turned and sipped from a ladle of water at hand, afterward dabbing at his mouth and beard with his sleeve. Finally, he spoke in a deep and gravelly voice.

"You've all heard the story of Tanegashima, for its events are justly famous. But today I'll reveal what no man's heard before—and speak to the wondrous power of collaboration."

Indeed, everyone present knew the history of Tanegashima, the green isle twenty-five miles south of Kyushu. But the listeners harkened close, for the blacksmith's bearing bespoke hard-won experience. Clearly this man had seen much of life.

"Years ago, one hot August day along Tanegashima's western shores, two peasants were combing the sands in the aftermath of a terrible storm, when a strange vessel with tattered sails drifted into view offshore.

"Fearing the arrival of a ghostship, the peasants ran to fetch Oribe, the village headman. Oribe and a party of villagers soon appeared on the beach. They found a longboat pulling onto the sand—and the boat's occupants caused them no small wonder.

"Five of the barbarians seemed to be from the Middle Kingdom, for they resembled the residents of Tanegashima in physique if not in dress. But two were red-haired, red-bearded giants, the likes of whom had never before been seen in Japan.

"These fiery-headed men wore the strangest of garments: knee-length pantaloons over black boots, sleeveless overshirts girded by thick brass-buckled belts, undershirts with puffed sleeves, and ruffled collars like *origami* rings. Atop their heads were wide black hats, behind which trailed plumes like those of some fanciful bird.

"One of the fiery-headed giants swept aside his elegant cape, doffed his hat, and executed a peculiar bow of greeting. The stunned villagers answered with formal bows in our style.

"Well, the giant began to speak in a tongue never before heard on Tanegashima—or anywhere else in Japan! The villagers, bewildered by his queer language, looked helplessly back and forth at each other. Finally, the fiery-headed one turned and uttered some words to the oldest of the Middle Kingdom castaways. This man stepped forward.

"'*Riben? Riben?*' he inquired, pointing to the ground beneath him.

"The man seemed to be the leader. Oribe shuffled forward to engage him. Using his cane like a brush, Oribe drew the characters for 'Japan' in the sand, then jabbed his left finger toward the earth. 'Japan! Japan!' he bellowed, as though shouting would clarify his meaning.

"This performance produced an amazing effect. The stranger clapped his hands and whooped, then grabbed Oribe's cane and sketched two ideographs in the sand. Pointing to his chest, he shouted, '*Zhongguo! Zhongguo!*' Oribe and several of his villagers nodded, smiling. The visitor had drawn the characters for 'Middle' and 'Kingdom.'

"Together the boat-men and the villagers pulled the launch farther onto the beach, then sat down upon the sand together. Oribe and the Chinese captain gestured, shouted, and drew characters, happy at each new understanding.

"The Chinese man called himself Wufeng. He explained with great difficulty that his junk, bound for Ningpo from Siam, had been seized by a terrible typhoon which sheared the sails and blew the ship relentlessly off course for more than twenty hours. Finally the vessel had floated into Tanegashima.

"Taking passage on Wufeng's ship were three Portuguese traders. Francisco—the one wearing blue pantaloons—was a chief merchant from the seaport of Malacca, trading between Malaysia, Macau, the Philippines, and China. Now these red-haired ones found themselves castaways in Japan, a land never before beheld by European eyes.

"Oribe sent a runner to deliver word of the newcomers to the prince of Tanegashima, the fifteen-year-old Tokitaka. Tokitaka, a smart and curious young man, promptly ordered the Chinese junk to be towed to the nearby port of Akaogi for repairs. The castaways should be given food and water, he instructed. Then, after an adequate period of rest, their leaders should be brought to the princely estate.

"By nightfall, Tanegashima buzzed with rumors about the mysterious vessel and its barbarian crew. At the castle, Tokitaka's advisers grumbled suspiciously about this Chinese who called himself Wufeng, for they believed he was actually the notorious pirate Wang Zhi. While Wufeng, the three Portuguese, and the ship's crew recuperated at the temple in Akaogi, Tokitaka's chief counselors cautioned the prince to regard these foreigners with the greatest suspicion.

"On the appointed day, the newcomers appeared at Tokitaka's estate. The Portuguese traders Francisco and Antonio stood by as Wufeng labored to retell the story of the typhoon and the landing at Tanegashima.

"Reposing in formal robes, young Tokitaka listened carefully, then asked from which nation the red-haired giants hailed. With much sign language and brush drawing, Wufeng managed to explain that Portugal lay far beyond the Middle Kingdom, through the Indian Ocean and around the great Horn of Africa. The red-haired merchants, he said, desired to trade with all the great kingdoms of the East.

"Tokitaka pointed to the arquebus held by Antonio. 'And is this one of the goods you offer for sale?'

"'No, that is a Portuguese weapon,' Wufeng replied.

"'A weapon? It looks duller than a bamboo pole. Does one use it to strike an opponent?'

"'It shoots a metal ball that fells one's enemy from a distance.'

"The young lord cocked his chin, puzzling.

"Antonio invited the prince to handle the device. As though examining something fallen from the sky, Tokitaka hefted the gun, turned it upside-down, and peered along its iron barrel. Then he held it in front of him, balancing it as he might a blade. The polished stock lay heavily in his hands, and its braided fuse arched out of the hammer mechanism like a snake poised to strike.

"'Show me,' the prince commanded.

"Tokitaka and his retainers stepped from the sitting room into the withering heat of the estate's gardens, lined with the miniature orange trees for which Satsuma Province is famous. One of Tokitaka's servants placed a large head of cabbage atop a bench, bowed, then quickly moved away. Another, carrying a lighted candle, hurried forward and stood at attention.

"Now Antonio gripped the arquebus and walked off counting aloud, the servant following behind. At a distance of forty paces from the bench, he stopped. Tokitaka watched, spellbound, as the red-haired merchant carefully pushed some queer gray powder and a lead ball down the barrel, then shook a quantity of the same powder onto the flashpan. With the servant's candle Antonio lit the gun's fuse, then looked to his host for a signal. Prince Tokitaka nodded.

"*Thoom!* A noise never before heard in Japan—like a thunderclap or a dozen trees felled at once—roared through the garden. A tongue of bright fire shot from the mouth of the foreign weapon. The cabbage exploded. Scraps of green and white vegetable matter fluttered through the air yards behind the bench.

"Peeking onto the scene through slatted *shoji* screens were a number of *kimono*-clad ladies in waiting. At the booming of the gun they shrieked and fled inside. A sulfurous smell hovered in the humid air.

"Tokitaka's attendants stared in mute awe at the pulped bits of cabbage. Their master tensed every muscle to keep from shouting out in alarm. The primitive musket's roar had triggered an explosive idea in the prince's young mind, a new conception he felt an overwhelming urge to realize immediately. He could not suppress his wonder.

"'Remarkable!' he exclaimed. 'Extraordinary for a

Collaboration Breeds Success: The Guns of Tanegashima 163

weapon to reach that distance with such power!'

"Wufeng cast a sly look at his red-haired friends. 'And it can destroy foes more formidable than vegetables,' he muttered in Portuguese, prompting sniggers from both.

"Again Tokitaka took the arquebus from Antonio. He turned it over and over in his hands, marveling. Smoke still wafted from the barrel. 'Francisco,' said the prince, 'will you sell me two of these guns?'

"For several minutes the two Portuguese conferred with Wufeng. Then the three nodded in agreement. 'One thousand pieces of silver each,' said the Chinese captain.

"Tokitaka's face flashed white with shock. Since the arrival of these strangers he'd shown only dignity and poise, but now he stammered. 'One thousand ... each? Too much. Offer a better price.'

"Wufeng and the traders murmured again, then both the Portuguese shook their heads. 'If one thousand's too much,' they said in their native tongue, 'you needn't buy.' The reply required no interpreting.

"Heated whispers arose among the prince's men. Every vassal knew their young lord was unused to having his wishes denied.

"Tokitaka breathed deeply and composed himself. 'I'd like to consult my advisers on this matter,' he said, and asked the foreign guests to retire to an anteroom. As the group dispersed, gardeners and servants rushed to clean up the grounds and restore the garden's shattered tranquility."

Here the blacksmith Goro paused for another ladle of water, for he was unaccustomed to speaking at such length. His listeners waited, the light of the temple's flickering oil lamps dancing upon their eager faces. Each student felt himself transported to the hot climes of the southern Kyushu kingdoms, where Satsuma warriors, renowned for their superb physiques, battled for supremacy.

Presently the old blacksmith resumed. The listeners strained to absorb every word.

"The *shoji* doors of Tokitaka's study slammed shut as the chief vassal, Kuronosuke, whirled to face his master. His balding head had reddened up to his topknot. 'Those ungrateful bandits! How dare they defile our hospitality with their greed!'

"'Easy now, Kuro,' said Tokitaka. 'Whatever their price, we should see this as an opportunity. The red-haired barbarians possess a science of weaponry far surpassing ours.'

"Fumio, the second senior retainer, spoke next. 'My Lord, these barbarians tell us they want to trade. But when they return, who's to say they won't bring a fleet of ships filled with warriors, each and every one armed with the wonder weapon? Or suppose they possess even bigger guns, and intend to colonize Japan?' He steadied himself before voicing his most worrisome thought. 'We must remember these Portuguese have come in convoy with a murderous pirate.'

"A tense silence descended upon the room. The prince and his advisers stared pensively at one another. Then Tokitaka turned to his martial arts instructor Ryu, or 'Dragon,' a squat, darkly complected man with eyes of black fire. 'Ryu, give your opinion of the Portuguese weapon.'

"'Formidable indeed. An army so equipped could be invincible. But that's what gives me pause.' Ryu frowned. 'May I speak freely, Lord Tokitaka?'

"'Of course.'

"'My Lord, I share your regard for this weaponry—but I'm also deeply troubled. The way of *Bushido* has always called for chivalrous engagement of one's enemy, a match of bravery and skill. The Portuguese device offers a tremendous advantage in warfare, no doubt. But to kill at such a distance, simply by lighting a wick ... Where is the skill in that? Where is the honor? If one clan adopts such a weapon, soon all will follow. What sort of world will we live in then? I say let the barbarians keep their barbaric arms.'

"Ryu's words gave pause. All thought silently for a long moment. Then Fumio spoke. 'I respect Ryu's sentiment, but Kuronosuke's right. How dare the foreigners try to weasel a profit out of us!' With a clenched fist he smacked the hilt of his *wakizashi* short sword. 'I say take the guns, sink that dragon-boat, and send the pirate Wang Zhi straight to hell where he belongs!'

"Lord Tokitaka leaned back on his *zabuton* cushion, arms folded and eyes closed in thought, a familiar posture that signaled the end of discussion. The young master would render a decision presently. For several long minutes the prince and his men sat silent, each recounting in his mind the hour's extraordinary events, each ominously aware that life in Japan would change after this day, in ways none could foretell.

"By and by, in an even-tempered voice, Tokitaka announced his conclusion. 'We will pay their outrageous price, and pay it gladly.' And before he could be urged otherwise, he raised a hand. 'Now hear me well. You've all given proper counsel, and your experience is greatly respected. Do not think my conclusion springs from the gullibility of youth.

"'The one called Wufeng may indeed be a bandit and a liar, and the red-haired barbarians greedy, ungrateful merchants. But that is not for us to judge. We lack direct knowledge of the pirate Wang Zhi, and these guns, even if commonplace elsewhere, have tremendous value in our islands. Surely the barbarians expect us to reproduce them. Thus they demand an exorbitant sum. They are selling us the science of these weapons, not merely two devices.'

"Accustomed though they were to Tokitaka's displays of keen wit, on this occasion the advisers marveled at how the youthful master's wisdom outshone their own.

"'Will the barbarians return to invade and plunder? Possibly. But a new era of dealings with other peoples has begun this day, with great likelihood of gain. Let us encourage our hopes, not our fears. Let us trust first, and have faith that our goodwill will beget trust in return. Let us collaborate, not conspire. To be sure, we could take the weapons by force and banish our uninvited guests—or slay them. But such a cowardly act would stain our honor for generations to come. And news of our treachery would invite the barbarians' vengeance.'

"Kuronosuke and Fumio reddened and lowered their eyes to the floor. Tokitaka turned to his martial master.

"'Ryu, your words are honorably spoken, and reveal your wisdom. I, too, fear the door we open today might never again be closed. But science has rendered weapons obsolete in the past. The sword, the spear, the glave—all have evolved over time. We must learn from the barbarians and their advanced industry. After all, the mechanisms of these fearsome guns may prove as useful for industry as for war.

"'For years, our Lord Shimazu has led the Satsuma Clan in fighting for control of Kyushu. If we learn to manufacture this new weapon in quantity, Shimazu will surely conquer our enemies at last and rule the entire isle. Extraordinary luck has washed onto Tanegashima's shores. Doesn't duty to Lord Shimazu demand we recognize this opportunity, conceive a clear goal to replicate these guns, and collaborate with the barbarians to achieve our aims?'

"So spoke young Lord Tokitaka. And so the Portuguese traders were paid two thousand pieces of silver for a brace of guns that would have fetched one-twentieth that price in Malacca. Francisco and Antonio left Japan praising the ill winds that had brought them there and vowing to return. Why bother trading with China and the Philippines when these enchanted isles of Japan promised wealth beyond imagining?

"And Lord Tokitaka? Well, history would prove the wisdom of his judgment. His chemist soon reproduced the Portuguese gunpowder. Screws, however, were unknown in Japan, and Kinbei, his blacksmith, was at first unable to find a method of fastening the lock and barrel mechanisms to a wooden stock. But the following year a Portuguese trade vessel docked at Tanegashima, and a friendly blacksmith aboard shared his secrets with Tokitaka's artisans.

"There was an apprentice in Kinbei's blacksmith shop at the time, a boy of sixteen. This young man beheld firsthand the remarkable effects of the trade relations established by Lord Tokitaka, relations that would bring far-reaching benefits to Japan. Soon this apprentice found himself very busy indeed. Thanks to that early collaboration with the Portuguese, Tanegashima became a center of firearms production."

Now Goro paused and held up both his hands, revealing a workman's rugged palms, thickly callused.

"Proud labor roughened these hands over many years, for I was that young apprentice. As Lord Tokitaka foresaw, the guns of Tanegashima changed Japan forever. Lord Shimazu indeed went on to conquer all of Kyushu. And as Hanshiro explained at a previous gathering, our guns have allowed Lord Nobunaga to unify half the nation."

Here the blacksmith concluded his tale. He had been talking for over an hour, and now seated himself among the students and took another drink of water. His story had inspired excited chatter in the audience.

Hideyoshi stepped forward and raised his hands, summoning quiet. "What lessons can we draw from the story of Tanegashima?"

A young peasant leapt to his feet, exclaiming, "We should keep the courage of our convictions, even in the face of opposing advice." Then, with a clever smile, he added, "Maybe vision and wisdom are not limited to the older and more experienced."

The students cheered.

A merchant spoke next. "Lord Tokitaka's wisdom lay in making allies rather than enemies of the red-haired giants. Thanks to his goodwill, the barbarians disclosed the secrets of the screw mechanism on their next visit. Two thousand pieces of silver for the guns was therefore a bargain." His glance roamed wishfully across the faces around him. "Would I could arrange such a profitable transaction!" He sat down amid knowing laughter.

Now the Portuguese trader Fernao rose to his feet. The knoll grew silent save for the squeaking of bats in the distance and the quiet ruffling of the evening breeze in the grass.

"I very grateful," said Fernao, "to merchants before me. They discover this great land and help make many tradings possible."

Fernao's hand moved thoughtfully in his beard. He stood silent a moment, attempting to summon the proper words, then spoke with conviction and care.

"But we Portuguese only visitors, and if tradings will happen, we must receive welcome of Japanese. Lord Tokitaka had many virtues, but curiosity was biggest with him. He think about more than science, more than foreign culture. He think about destiny, man's place in this world! His story teaches us of learning from strangers—and how good tradings begin. Surely, like Sir Hideyoshi say, *Collaboration Breeds Success.*"

Sounds of agreement rippled across the knoll.

Now there was a commotion at the rear of the assembly. Heads turned as the peasants Jiro and Gonsuke jumped up together with Daizen, the *ronin*.

"Speaking of collaboration," shouted Jiro, "we have an announcement!"

The trio made their way through the crowd toward the speaking stump. Daizen gripped a wooden *bokuto* practice sword in one hand.

Reaching the front, Jiro turned to face the rows of students. "Friends, it's barely two months since my comrade Gonsuke and I traveled from Miwa Village to Nagahama to seek Sir Hideyoshi's advice on achieving prosperity—yet now that seems a lifetime ago. The journey has been fruitful beyond our wildest imaginings. Master Hideyoshi, from the depths of our hearts, we thank you for your wisdom, your generosity, and your gracious good humor."

The knoll roared with shouts of assent.

"Hear! Hear!"

"Cheers for Master Hideyoshi!"

The threesome raised their hands for quiet, then Jiro leapt atop the speaking stump. He was holding a carved walking staff.

"Thanks to Sir Hideyoshi's inspiration, we're all better prepared to seek prosperity and fulfillment," he cried. "As for me, I've gained faith in my carpentry skills."

Jiro raised the staff high in one hand, and every student beheld an exquisite likeness of *Benten,* the goddess of luck, carved in the staff's polished maple. The superb workmanship drew murmurs of admiration as Jiro turned to present the beautiful object to Hideyoshi. With a show of dignified emotion, the great teacher accepted the gift, touching a silken handkerchief to his eyes.

Gonsuke jumped up beside Jiro. "Sir Hideyoshi's

teachings likewise gave me faith in my knack for trade," he added. "So I've founded a business to sell Jiro's furniture and carvings. Who can better appraise the beauty and value of my friend's woodwork, and urge its purchase by others? Over the past two months we've labored day and night to design merchandise both beautiful and practical. Our failures were many, but as Sir Hideyoshi taught us, we redoubled our efforts to achieve extraordinary results."

The peasants hopped down from the stump as Daizen sprang atop it. His voice shook with emotion.

"As we heard tonight, Master Hideyoshi's final secret is *Collaboration Breeds Success*. For a loner like me, this was the hardest lesson of all. But today I'm happy to announce that I've joined Jiro and Gonsuke in their venture, and we will produce, among other items, the finest practice swords, made to my exacting specifications!"

Whereupon Gonsuke tossed the *ronin* a second wooden sword, and Daizen whipped the two *bokuto* through the air like mere feathers, twirling them about his head and body. They appeared to come alive and dance by a power all their own, blurring like the play of a dozen swords. The students roared with admiration and glee.

"With these practice weapons and my expertise in their demonstration," the *ronin* proclaimed, "we will gain customers among samurai and noble households—lucrative outlets for our other products!"

At this, Daizen flung one *bokuto* high, then the other, and launched himself off the stump into a flying somersault, coming down on two feet to catch the weapons with a triumphant flourish.

The studentship erupted into thunderous applause. The three partners bowed and started back to their places, but were thronged by joyous classmates who'd jumped up to wish them well and admire Daizen's swords.

Now, for the last time, Hideyoshi clambered atop the speaking stump and signaled for quiet. "Jiro, Gonsuke, Daizen—you've provided a most fitting close to our lessons."

The samurai lifted his new walking staff, and the burnished maple figure of the goddess *Benten* seemed to hover, gleaming, in the lamplight.

"May you all attract good luck in the promising days ahead, for the age of strife is ending and a new era of promise is dawning."

Amid a tremendous huzzah, the giant Koroku appeared and whisked the merry samurai through the crowd, till the pair vanished beyond the Soganji Temple grounds.

As night drew down upon the temple knoll, a host of students lingered in spirited discussion. They felt the powerful truth of Hideyoshi's final words. To be sure, now was a time of promise. Change was in the air—for Japan itself, as for each man who heeded the samurai's secrets of fortune and fulfillment.

And indeed, just a few short years hence, every student of the temple school would witness the feats of a new leader whose vision transcended mere conquest. This man embraced a dream to reunite a war-torn nation and launch a new age of peace and prosperity. He would achieve this vision, earning himself an immortal place in history. Tales of his successes would echo through the centuries, and all who heard them would marvel that so great a man was born a humble peasant. His name was Hideyoshi.

Hideyoshi and the Age of Warring Clans

Toyotomi Hideyoshi was a real person—and one of the world's most extraordinary men. He was born in 1536 or 1537 in the farming village of Nakamura, now a suburb of Nagoya, where the Toyota Motor Corporation is based. Little is certain about Hideyoshi's life before he began working for Oda Nobunaga at age eighteen, but the history presented in this book reflects popular consensus about his early days. One point is certain: he was born a peasant, with little to his name.

Hideyoshi rose swiftly within the Oda clan and committed himself wholeheartedly to Nobunaga's ambitious quest to conquer Japan's warring fiefdoms and reunite the nation "under a single sword." He replaced Nobunaga after the latter's assassination in 1582, and by 1590 controlled most of the nation.

After Hideyoshi's death in 1598, Japan's unification was completed under Tokugawa Ieyasu.

Hideyoshi, though much less dashing than Nobunaga or Ieyasu, is the man who has most inspired ordinary Japanese citizens to believe in their own abilities. Unlike his privileged peers, Hideyoshi "pulled himself up by the bootstraps." Despite his small size, scant martial gifts, and impoverished beginnings, he rose to become Japan's supreme political and military leader and the Emperor's proxy. His success was self-willed, his life an Horatio Alger-like rags-to-riches adventure.

Hideyoshi's story dramatically captures the very essence of Japan's Age of Warring Clans, the extraordinary years between the late 1400s and early 1600s. During this period, in the absence of a central government, provincial lords were obliged to survive by their own resourcefulness and talent lest they be overthrown by stronger leaders—or more powerful armies. The tumultuous era gave rise to the term *gekokujo*, meaning "the low supplanting the high-and-mighty," a new shorthand for the fledgling meritocracy emerging within Japan's feudal society. In most cases, however, those who rose amid the tumult of *gekokujo* were not truly "low": they were samurai, influential merchants, or ambitious deputy governors—rather than poor farmers. Hideyoshi's astonishing ascendance therefore carried a special poignancy for unprivileged commoners who longed to best their superiors.

No other era has captured Japan's popular imagination like the Age of Warring Clans, when warlords battled over some five dozen fiefdoms, bandits and *ronin* roamed the countryside, and hard-bitten samurai—both gallant and devious—won immortal fame. It was the country's defining moment, one blood-drenched and chaotic but rich in promise, whose colorful lore recalls both the American Wild West and Europe's days of Arthur. Yet the Age of Warring Clans has proven more profoundly influential than those western counterparts: four centuries after Hideyoshi's death, the image and ideals of the samurai remain vital in Japan.

The Age of Warring Clans marked astonishing leaps in industry and the arts, and the first contact with European peoples. It's interesting to note that Japan's three great unifiers—Nobunaga, Hideyoshi, and Ieyasu—were all born within nine years of each other, and in close geographic proximity, in an area known for extraordinary craftsmanship. These three—and Hideyoshi in particular—laid the foundation for the Japan we know today. As the nation's supreme leader, Hideyoshi restored peace, built roads, bridges, and other social infrastructure, instituted a comprehensive program of land reform, constructed a surprisingly autonomous system of distributed governance, promoted artistic and cultural development, and refurbished the pomp and decorum of the long neglected royal family.

Hideyoshi did not formally expound the Five Secrets contained in this book, but they can be inferred from the edicts and decrees he left behind, and his life seemed to illustrate them naturally. Gratitude, knowledge of his gifts, conception of achievable goals, exertion of extraordinary effort, and effective collaboration enabled this tiny man of common birth to command a nation and become its most prosperous "peasant." One might imagine that similar values enabled Japan, a resource-scarce island country, to develop into the world's second greatest economic superpower.

But perhaps there is a final secret behind Hideyoshi's and Japan's success, one to be found within the *Bushido* code of the samurai. In our final chapter, we'll leave you to contemplate the *Bushido* virtues that, sadly, seem increasingly scarce in today's world.

Bushido

An abridgement of the text by Nitobe Inazo

Bu-shi-do means literally Military-Knight-Ways: the ways samurai should behave in both professional and daily life. In other words, *Bushido* was the code of moral principles samurai were required to observe. It was not a written code, nor was it the creation of a single person. It evolved organically over centuries of military history and found its purest expression in Japan's feudal period (1185-1868).

As in Europe, feudalism in Japan gave birth to a professional class of warriors. These warriors were known as samurai, meaning guards or attendants of royalty. Samurai were recruited from the strongest and most adventurous men over a long period of constant warfare. In time, the less able were weeded out, with only the strongest surviving to form samurai families.

Samurai claimed great honor and privilege—and correspondingly great responsibilities—so these warriors soon felt the need for a common standard of chivalrous behavior, as well as a code of civil conduct to refer to when punishing wrongdoing among their own.

Japan's intellectual and moral culture was thus created by the samurai and their code. There was no channel of human activity, no avenue of thought, which *Bushido* did not influence or inspire. *Bushido* remains the animating spirit of the country. Being unwritten, it's a code expressed only in genuine deeds, a law inscribed nowhere but on the fleshly tablets of the heart.

Bushido's first source was Buddhism, which furnished a sense of calm trust in Fate, a quiet submission to the inevitable, a stoic composure when faced with danger or calamity, a belief that life brings suffering and that death needn't be feared.

What Buddhism failed to give, Shintoism—Japan's native religion incorporating the worship of ancestors and nature spirits—offered in abundance. Shinto doctrines taught loyalty to the emperor, reverence for ancestral memory, and brotherliness, imparting dignity and gentility to the otherwise arrogant character of the samurai.

As for ethical doctrines, the teachings of Confucius were the most prolific source of *Bushido*. His articulation of the five moral relations—master to servant, father to son, husband to wife, older brother to younger, friend to friend—served to confirm what the Japanese had recognized instinctively before his writings were introduced from China. And Confucius's aristocratic, conservative tone fit in well with the samurai, who were warrior statesmen. The writings of Confucius and Mencius were the principal textbooks for youths and served as the highest authority in discussions amongst the old.

Mere acquaintance with the teachings of these two sages was held, however, in no high esteem. A common Japanese proverb ridicules the person who possesses only an intellectual knowledge of Confucius; such a person is a studious but ignorant man.

Bushido made light of 'knowledge for knowledge's sake.' It should not be pursued as an end in itself, but as a means to the attainment of wisdom. He who stopped short of wisdom was regarded no higher than a convenient machine, which could turn out poems and maxims at bidding. A typical samurai calls a literary savant a 'book-smelling sot'; another compares learning to a reeking vegetable that requires thorough boiling before it's fit for use. A man who has read a little smells a little bookish, and a man who has read much smells much more so, and both are unpleasant. True knowledge comes only when one's learning is assimilated in one's mind and displayed in one's character. Ethical emotion is more important than intellect.

Thus, knowledge was not separated from its practical application in life; the Chinese philosopher, Wan Yang Ming never wearied of repeating, "To know and to act are one and the same."

The essential virtues of *Bushido* were few and

simple. They ensured a samurai's survival even in the most tumultuous period of Japanese history: The Age of Warring Clans.

The Eight Virtues of Bushido

I. Rectitude or Justice

Rectitude or Justice, is the strongest virtue of *Bushido*. A well-known samurai defines it this way: "Rectitude is one's power to decide upon a course of conduct in accordance with reason, without wavering; to die when to die is right, to strike when to strike is right."

Another speaks of it in the following terms: "Rectitude is the bone that gives firmness and stature. Without bones the head cannot rest on top of the spine, nor hands move nor feet stand. So without Rectitude neither talent nor learning can make the human frame into a samurai."

Nothing is more loathsome to the samurai than underhanded dealings and crooked undertakings. During the Age of Warring Clans, when cunning and trickery could pass for military tact, and downright falsehood for strategy, the manly virtue of Rectitude was the jewel that shone brightest and was most highly praised. A *Gishi* (a man of Rectitude) was considered superior to any master of learning or art. Rectitude is a twin brother to Courage.

 ## II. Courage

Courage is worthy of being counted among virtues only if it's exercised in the cause of Righteousness and Rectitude. In his Analects, Confucius says: "Perceiving what is right and doing it not reveals a lack of Courage." In short, "Courage is doing what is right."

To risk danger, to jeopardize one's self, to rush into the jaws of death—these are too often identified with Courage, and in the warrior profession such rashness is often unjustly applauded; but not so in *Bushido*. Death for an unworthy cause is called a "dog's death." "To rush into the thick of battle and to be slain in it," wrote a Prince of Mito, "is easy enough, and any oaf is equal to the task. True Courage is to live when it's right to live, and die only when it's right to die."

Courage, Valor, Fortitude, Bravery, Fearlessness are qualities of soul that can be learned by exercise and example, and thus were the most popular virtues among the youth of historical Japan. Almost before he left his mother's breast, a boy was familiar with stories of military exploits. Should he cry at the slightest ache, his mother would scold him: "What a coward to cry for a trifling pain! What will you do when your arm is cut off in battle? What will you do when you are called upon to commit *harakiri* (ritual suicide by disembowelment with a sword)?"

Anecdotes of fortitude and bravery abound in nursery tales. Parents, with sternness sometimes verging on cruelty, set children to tasks that called forth all their pluck. "Bears hurl their cubs down the gorge," these parents said, so samurai sons were pushed down the steep valleys of hardship. Occasional deprivation of food or exposure to cold were considered good ways to build endurance and Courage. Young children were sent among utter strangers with some message to deliver, made to rise before the sun and do their reading exercises, or walk to their lessons barefooted in the cold of winter. Pilgrimages to all sorts of fearful places—execution grounds, graveyards, houses reputed to be haunted—were favorite pastimes of the young. In the days when decapitations were performed publicly, not only were small boys sent to witness the ghastly scenes, but they were made to visit the execution place alone in the darkness of night and leave a mark of their visit on the severed head.

Courage creates the spiritual trait of composure, or calm presence of mind. In other words, composure is Courage at rest. A truly brave man is ever serene; he is never taken by surprise; nothing ruffles the equanimity of his spirit. In the heat of battle he remains cool; in the midst of catastrophe he thinks clearly.

Earthquakes do not shake him, he laughs at storms. The one who retains his self-possession in the presence of mortal danger is admired as truly great—the one, for instance, who can compose a poem under impending peril or can hum a tune in the face of death. Such composure is an infallible sign of a large nature—of a great mind.

Courage and Honor require that we should battle in war only those enemies worthy of being friends in peace. When Courage attains this height, it becomes akin to Benevolence.

III. Benevolence or Mercy

Love, magnanimity, affection for others, sympathy and pity, are traits of Benevolence, the highest attribute of the human soul. Both Confucius and Mencius often said the highest requirement of a ruler of men is Benevolence.

Confucius writes, "Let but a prince cultivate virtue, people will flock to him; with people will come to him lands; lands will bring him wealth; wealth will give him the benefit of right uses. Virtue is the root, and wealth an outcome."

Mercy, or Benevolence toward the weak, the downtrodden or the defeated, was always held as the highest manifestation of the samurai's noble spirit. *"Bushi no nasake*"—the tenderness of a warrior—appealed to the inherent decency in mankind. A samurai's Mercy was not different from the mercy of anyone else, but *Bushido* emphasized Mercy as something more than a blind impulse, Mercy as a due regard for Justice—and backed with the power to save or kill.

Benevolence and the cultivation of tender feelings breeds considerate regard for the suffering of others. Such regard for others' feelings is at the root of Politeness.

 ## IV. Politeness

Courtesy and good manners have been noticed by every foreign tourist as distinctive Japanese traits. But Politeness should be the expression of a benevolent regard for the feelings of others; it's a poor virtue if it's motivated only by a fear of offending good taste. In its highest form Politeness approaches love.

Foreigners often ridicule the elaborate Japanese discipline of Politeness, claiming it absorbs too much thought and wastes too much effort of those who observe strict obedience to it. While there may be unnecessary niceties in Japanese etiquette, it's unclear whether such strict observance in Japan absorbs as much thought and wastes as much effort as does a Westerner's adherence to ever-changing fashions.

Fashions in the West can be seen as a ceaseless search of the human mind for the beautiful. Certainly an elaborate Japanese ceremony is no more trivial.

Ceremonies develop from long practice. If something is to be done, there's certainly a best way to do it, and the most appropriate method evolves slowly over the centuries until it becomes a ceremony. The more graceful the method the better, for gracefulness can be defined as the most economical expenditure of motion. The tea ceremony involves precise ways of manipulating a bowl, a spoon, a napkin, and so forth. To a novice it looks tedious. But one soon discovers that the way prescribed saves time and labor; in other words, the most economical movements are used, and they are therefore the most graceful.

Thus the tea ceremony shows how the simplest thing can be made into an art and then become spiritual culture. Tea-sipping as a spiritual practice? Why not? Calmness of mind, serenity of temper, composure and quietness of demeanor, which are all essentials to the tea ceremony, are the first conditions of right thinking and right feeling, which breed true Politeness.

The very fact that the tea ceremony was invented by a contemplative Hindu hermit in a time when wars and the rumors of wars were incessant shows that this institution was more than a pastime. Before entering the quiet precincts of the tearoom, participants laid their swords aside, along with the ferocity of the battlefield or the intrigues of government. In the tea-room they found peace and friendship.

Politeness is a treasure even if it does nothing more than lend grace to manners, but its function does not stop there. For Politeness is an expression of sympathy. It requires that we weep with those who weep, and rejoice with those who rejoice. In the details of everyday life, this sympathy expresses itself in little acts that may appear, as a foreign missionary lady of twenty years' residence once said, "awfully funny."

Suppose you are out in the hot glaring sun without shade. A Japanese acquaintance passes by. You greet him, and instantly his hat is off. Well, that's perfectly natural, but the "awfully funny" thing is that the whole time he talks with you, his parasol is down and he stands in the glaring sun also. How foolish! Yes, it would be, if his motive were less than this: "You are in the sun; I sympathize with you; I would willingly take you under my parasol if it were large enough, or if we were familiarly acquainted; since I cannot shade you, I will share your discomfort." Little acts of this kind are not mere gestures or conventionalities. They are the embodiment of sympathy, of thoughtful feelings for the comfort of others.

Another "awfully funny" thing is dictated by Japanese customs of Politeness. In America, when you give a gift, you sing its praises to the recipient; in Japan you depreciate or slander it. The underlying idea in America is, "This is a nice gift: if it were not nice I would not give it to you, for it would be an insult to give you anything but what is nice." In contrast, Japanese logic runs: "You are a nice person, and no gift is nice enough for you. You will not accept anything I can lay at your feet except as a token of my good will, so accept this not for its intrinsic value but as a token. It would be an insult to your worth to call the best gift good enough for you." Place the two customs side by side, and we see that the idea is one and the same. Neither is "awfully funny." The American speaks of the material that makes the gift; the Japanese speaks of the spirit that prompts the gift.

V. Honesty and Sincerity

Without Honesty and Sincerity, Politeness is a farce and a show. "Politeness exaggerated," wrote Masamune, "becomes a lie." And Confucius wrote: "Sincerity is the end and the beginning of all things; without Sincerity there would be nothing." Confucius spoke of Sincerity's power to produce change without movement, to accomplish its purpose effortlessly, through its mere presence. In Chinese, one writes "Sincerity" by combining the characters for "Word" and "Perfect."

To the samurai, lying or equivocation were deemed

cowardly. The word of a samurai sufficiently guaranteed the truthfulness of his assertion. A samurai's word carried such weight, in fact, that promises were generally made and fulfilled without a written pledge, which would have been quite beneath his dignity. Many thrilling anecdotes tell of those who atoned for *nigon* (a double tongue) by death.

The samurai believed his high social position demanded a higher standard of Honesty than that of the tradesman and peasant. Of all the occupations in life, none was farther removed from the profession of arms than commerce. The samurai disdained money, both making it and hoarding it. They believed in the precept that: "Men must grudge money, for riches hinder wisdom." Hence samurai children were brought up with utter disregard for financial matters. It was considered bad taste to speak of money. Ignorance of the value of different coins showed good breeding. Knowledge of numbers was indispensable in the mustering of forces, as in the distribution of territories and fiefs; but the counting of money was left to inferiors. Public finance was often administered by a lower samurai or by a priest. Every thinking samurai knew very well that money formed the sinews of war; but he would never consider raising the appreciation of money to a virtue.

Bushido encouraged thrift, not for economical reasons so much as for the exercise of abstinence. Luxury was thought the greatest menace to manhood, and severe simplicity was required of the warrior class. The samurai earned his income from land and could even indulge in amateur farming if he had a mind to; but the counting machine and abacus were abhorred. This social arrangement kept the distribution of wealth more equitable, preventing riches from accumulating solely in the hands of the powerful.

Money and the love of it being diligently ignored, *Bushido* remained free from the thousand and one evils of which money is the root. This is the reason our public men have long avoided corruption (but, alas, how quickly a government of the rich is establishing itself in our time and generation!).

Those who are well acquainted with Japanese history will remember that feudalism was abolished only a few years after our ports were opened to foreign trade. The samurai's fiefs were taken and bonds issued in compensation. The samurai were suddenly at liberty to invest in the marketplace. Many a noble and honest warrior irrevocably failed in his new trade through sheer lack of shrewdness in coping with his artful rival, the common merchant. Many fortunes were wrecked in the attempt to apply *Bushido* ethics to business methods. It was obvious to every observing mind that the ways of wealth were not the ways of Honor.

 ## VI. Honor

The sense of Honor, a vivid consciousness of personal dignity and worth, characterized the samurai. He was born and bred to value the duties and privileges of his profession. Fear of disgrace hung like a sword over the head of every samurai.

Bushido instilled magnanimity and patience. To take offense at slight provocation was ridiculed as "short-tempered." As the popular adage put it: "True patience means bearing the unbearable." The great Ieyasu left to posterity a few maxims, among which are the following: "Reproach none, but be forever watchful of thine own short-comings ... Forbearance is the basis of length of days." He proved in his life the truth of what he preached.

The heights of meekness and patience that *Bushido* encouraged—seemingly at odds with the samurai's martial ways—may also be seen in this saying of Ogawa: "When others speak evil things against thee, return not evil for evil, but rather reflect that thou wast not more faithful in the discharge of thy duties." This sentiment is echoed by Kumazawa: "When others blame thee, blame them not; when others are angry at thee, return not anger. Joy cometh only as Passion and Desire part." Lastly, Saigo puts it this way: "With the love wherewith thou lovest thyself, love others ... Never condemn others; but see to it that thou comest not short of thine own mark." Some of these sayings remind us of Christian expostulations. And they did not remain mere sayings, but were embodied in acts.

Samurai boys found it hard to forget that Honor won in youth grows with age. In the memorable siege of Osaka, a young son of Ieyasu, in spite of his earnest requests to be put in the front line, was placed at the rear. When the castle fell he wept so bitterly that an old councilor tried to console him: "Take comfort, Sire, at thought of the long future before you. In the many years that you may live, there will come diverse occasions to distinguish yourself."

The boy fixed his indignant gaze upon the man and said: "How foolishly you talk! Can ever my fourteenth year come round again?"

Life itself was thought cheap compared to the Honor and fame one might attain: hence, whenever a cause presented itself that was considered dearer than life, with serenity and quickness life was laid down.

In considering the *Bushido* virtue of Honor, readers should understand that the infamous samurai practice of *seppuku*, also known as *harakiri*, was no mere act of suicide, but an institution, both legal and ceremonial. Invented in the middle ages, ritual suicide was a warrior's means of expiating crimes, apologizing for errors, escaping from disgrace, redeeming his friends, and proving his Sincerity. When enforced as a legal punishment, it was carried out with due ceremony. It served to refine one's self-destruction, and a samurai could perform it only with the utmost composure and coolness of temper. For all these reasons it was particularly befitting the profession of the samurai.

Naturally, the glorification of *seppuku* created the temptation to commit suicide in unnecessary or irresponsible ways. For causes entirely irrational, or for reasons entirely undeserving of death, hotheaded youths rushed into suicide as moths to the flame; mixed and dubious motives drove more samurai to this deed than nuns through convent gates.

From this bloody practice, as well as from the general tenor of *Bushido*, it's easy to infer that the sword played an important part in Japanese social discipline and life. It's true that the sword was referred to as the 'soul of the samurai,' and the same weapon was seen as an emblem of power and prowess. True, also, that very early in life the samurai boy learned to wield his sword, and in a momentous occasion at the age of five he was dressed in the paraphernalia of the samurai, placed upon a *go* board and initiated into the rights of the military profession by having a real sword thrust into his belt, instead of the toy dagger with which he'd been playing. When he reached manhood at fifteen and gained full independence, a samurai son could pride himself upon the possession of arms sharp enough for any battle. The very possession of the dangerous instrument imparted a feeling of self-respect and responsibility.

Furthermore, the swordsmith was no mere craftsman but an inspired artist, and his workshop a sanctuary. Daily he began his work with prayer and purification, or, as the phrase went, "he committed his soul and spirit into the forging and tempering of the steel." Every swing of the sledge, every plunge into water, every friction on the grindstone, was a religious act.

The question that concerns us most is: Did *Bushido* justify the promiscuous wielding of the sword? The answer is unequivocally, no! Instead, *Bushido* laid great stress on a sword's proper purpose, and denounced its misuse. Only a foolish braggart brandished his weapon on undeserved occasions. A self-possessed man knew the right time to use it, and knew that such times came only rarely.

VII. Loyalty

Loyalty to a superior was the most distinctive virtue of the feudal era. Personal fidelity exists among all sorts of men: a gang of pickpockets swears allegiance to its leader. But only in the code of chivalrous Honor does Loyalty assume paramount importance.

One of the most loyal characters in our history is the man in the following story:

Due to the jealousy and corruption around him, the noble Lord Michizane found himself exiled from his capital. Not content with merely banishing the lord, Michizane's unrelenting enemies plotted to destroy his family. A search for his son—a boy not yet grown—revealed the child being hidden in a village school kept by Genzo, Michizane's former vassal. The schoolmaster was ordered to deliver the head of the boy.

Receiving the terrible command, Genzo's first idea was to find a convincing substitute for the young noble's head. He pondered his roster of students, scrutinized all the boys as they strolled into his classroom, but none among the children bore the least resemblance to his protégé. His despair, however, was only momentary for, behold, a new scholar soon arrived—a boy of the same age as his master's son, escorted by a mother of noble mien. This mother and the boy himself were fully conscious of his resemblance to the lord's son. In the privacy of their home the boy and mother had pledged full faithfulness to Michizane, so when the schoolmaster proposed his plan, an agreement was made between the three. Here, then, was a willing sacrifice!

On the day appointed, an officer arrived to retrieve the head of the youth. Would he be deceived? The officer took up the gruesome object and pored calmly over each feature. Poor Genzo's hand was on the hilt of his sword, ready to strike a blow either at the officer or at himself, should the examination reveal his scheme. But then, in a deliberate, business-like tone, the officer pronounced the head genuine.

That evening, in her lonely home, the mother of the dead schoolboy waited. Did she know the fate of her child? It was not for his return that she watched with eagerness. Her husband's father had long been a favorite of Michizane's, but since the lord's banishment, circumstances had forced her husband to serve Michizane's enemy. He himself could not be untrue to his own cruel master, but his son could serve the cause of the kinder lord. As one acquainted with the exile's family, it was he who'd been charged with the task of identifying the boy's head. Now the day's hard work was done and he returned home, saying: "Rejoice, my wife, our darling son has proved of service to his lord!"

"What an atrocious story!" I hear the reader exclaim. "Parents deliberately sacrificing their own innocent child to save the life of another man's." But this child was a conscious and willing victim: it is a story of noble death—as significant as, and no more revolting than, the story of Abraham's intended sacrifice of Isaac. Both tales portray obedience to the call of Loyalty—whether voiced by a visible or an invisible angel, or heard by an outward or an inward ear.

The individualism of the West, which believes in separate interests for father, son, husband and wife, emphasizes the duties each one owes to the other;

but *Bushido* held that the interests of each family member were inseparable from the interests of the family as a whole.

 ## VIII. Character and Self-Control

The first objective of samurai education was to build up Character. The subtler faculties of prudence, intelligence, and dialectics were less important. Intellectual superiority was esteemed, but a samurai was essentially a man of action. Science was outside the pale of his interests. He took advantage of it only to the degree that it related to his profession of arms. Religion and theology were relegated to the priests; the samurai concerned himself with them only to the degree that they helped nourish his Courage. Philosophy and literature comprised most of his intellectual training; but even in these pursuits, it was not objective truth he sought. Literature was pursued mainly as a pastime, and philosophy as a practical aid in the formation of Character.

When a teacher seeks to sharpen Character and not intelligence, the soul and not the brain, his vocation takes on a sacred quality. "It's the parent who has borne me: it's the teacher who makes me a man." With this idea, one's teacher was held in very high esteem. He was a father to the fatherless, and an adviser to the erring. Because the samurai code promoted service for honor's sake, rather than financial gain, the spiritual service of a teacher was never repaid in gold or silver, not because this service was valueless, but because it was invaluable. Wages and salaries could be paid only for services whose results were definite, tangible, and measurable. The noblest goal of education was to improve the soul, and since such improvement could not be quantified, it could not be repaid with money.

Pupils did bring money or goods to their teachers at different seasons of the year; these were not payments, though, but offerings, and were welcomed by the recipients, who were usually men of honorable poverty, too dignified to work with their hands and too proud to beg. These moneyless teachers were undaunted by adversity. They embodied what was considered the highest end of all learning, and were thus living examples of that discipline of disciplines, Self-Control, which was universally required of samurai.

It was considered unmanly for a samurai to betray his emotions. "He shows no sign of joy or anger," was a phrase used to describe a strong Character. The most natural affections were kept under control. A father could embrace his son only at the expense of his dignity; a husband would not kiss his wife in the presence of other people, whatever he might do in private! Self-Control was not to be disturbed by passion of any kind.

During the late war with China, when a regiment

left a certain town, a large crowd of people flocked to the station to bid farewell to the general and his army. On this occasion an American resident was present, expecting to witness loud demonstrations, for the nation itself was highly excited and there were fathers, mothers, and sweethearts of the soldiers in the crowd. The American was disappointed. As the whistle blew and the train began to move, thousands of people silently removed their hats and bowed their heads in reverential farewell; no waving of handkerchiefs, no word uttered, but deep silence in which only an attentive ear could catch a few broken sobs.

Bushido's disciplines combine to create a stoical turn of mind, and discipline in Self-Control can easily go too far. It can repress the genial current of the soul. It can beget bigotry, breed hypocrisy, or dull one's affections. Yet the Japanese are really as susceptible to tender emotion as any people under the sun. Every *Bushido* virtue has its counterpart and counterfeit. We must recognize the positive excellence of each virtue and strive to follow it positively.

What Japan was and is, she owes to the samurai. The virtues of *Bushido* have served for centuries as the foundation of the country's enduring prosperity. And it is *Bushido*'s inarguable wisdom, relevant to every age, that ensures Japan's vitality despite the enormous challenges she faces today. So long as humans seek to better themselves and their circumstances, so long as opportunity and ennoblement are sought, *Bushido* will resonate.

In a strictly historical sense, the samurai never existed who managed to live wholly and unfailingly by the ideals of this code of chivalry—Hideyoshi being no exception. Nevertheless *Bushido's* moral tenets, like guiding rays from the heavens, remain worthy beacons for anyone who wishes to achieve success without sacrificing character, to attain fortune while remaining generous and merciful, and to gain that most priceless of treasures, the truest measure of prosperity: fulfillment.

Afterword

The Prosperous Peasant is a work of fiction. Much of the story, however, is based on actual events that occurred during Toyotomi Hideyoshi's lifetime (1536?-1598), and we've striven to be faithful to history and to what is known of Hideyoshi's life and personality.

Hideyoshi's temple school is pure invention, and was inspired by George Clason's classic work, *The Richest Man in Babylon*. We acknowledge a tremendous debt to Mr. Clason and his extraordinary book, whose influence can be seen most clearly in Chapter 4, "The Temple School," which we've modeled directly on Clason's chapter entitled "Meet the Goddess of Good Luck."

Chapters 1 through 6 of *The Prosperous Peasant* are mostly fictional, though Hideyoshi and his attendant Koroku were real people and the locales and key events described are fair to history. Several paragraphs of text adapted from Walter Dening's *The Life of Toyotomi Hideyoshi* are quoted in Chapter 5, and the final third of that chapter incorporates text from the short story *Honest Kyūsuke* by Miyamori Asataro. Chapter 8 is an adapted version of the short story entitled *Ungo-*

Zenji, also by Miyamori. We've changed names and locales, but have utilized most of Miyamori's original text. Chapters 7 and 9 recount actual historical episodes, with fictional dialogue and some invented characters. Chapter 11 is an abridgement of *Bushido* by Nitobe Inazo, edited from roughly 33,000 words down to approximately 5,000, modified with modern punctuation and vocabulary. We've manipulated Nitobe's phrasing in many places, and have incorporated our own concluding paragraph. Readers are encouraged to refer to the full text of *Bushido,* which is freely available online.

We thank Kitami Masao for first teaching us about Hideyoshi, and James Reid Harrison for his contributions to Chapters 1 and 9 and for his thorough and professional copyediting of the entire manuscript.

Readers and historians knowledgeable about the Age of Warring Clans might well object to the rather rosy portrait of Hideyoshi painted here. The authors are fully aware of the dark side of Hideyoshi's later career (foreshadowed in Chapter 3), and encourage those interested to read *The Swordless Samurai*, author Clark's previous work based on Hideyoshi's life (SwordlessSamurai.com).

We recognize that many readers will be unfamiliar with the Japanese language, so in selecting fictional character names we favored readability over regional authenticity or other concerns. To this end we chose not to use macrons (such as ū or ō). Japanophiles and history buffs may register complaints at TheProsperousPeasant.com.

A bibliography of several dozen Japanese and English language sources used in the research and writing of this book can be viewed at TheProsperousPeasant.com/book/sources/. For basic facts and interpretations we relied heavily on works such as *Hideyoshi no Subete ga Wakaru Hon* by Professor Owada Tetsuo of Shizuoka University, who is widely acknowledged in Japan as the foremost scholar of Hideyoshi's life. Nevertheless, as Professor Owada himself asserts, Hideyoshi's legacy is so tightly intertwined with romantic legend that it's impossible to claim historical accuracy in representing many aspects of his life.

But perhaps that's the very reason Hideyoshi is so appealing. We hope you will derive as much pleasure—and as much inspiration—from his story as we have.

Tim Clark and Mark Cunningham
Portland, Oregon ✿ September 2007

About the authors

Tim Clark is a Portland, Oregon-based entrepreneur, writer, and teacher. He spent ten years in Japan and worked as a translator and technology industry commentator before founding a consultancy that was acquired by a NASDAQ-listed company. Today he teaches entrepreneurship courses and is pursuing a doctoral degree in international business through Hitotsubashi University. *The Prosperous Peasant* is his third book. Please visit TimClark.net.

Mark Allen Cunningham is a Portland, Oregon-based novelist. His newest novel is *Lost Son*, based on the life and work of the European poet Rainer Maria Rilke. Cunningham's first novel, *The Green Age of Asher Witherow* was cited as one of six "Best Books of the West" by the Salt Lake Tribune and was shortlisted for the BookSense Book of the Year Award in 2005. He has published numerous short stories. Please visit MAllenCunningham.com.

TheProsperousPeasant.com

Pg 115 Attention
143 endurance